Contents

Introduction

A lifetime of excitment awaits you and your dog, so let us show you how to ensure the happiness and health of your canine best friend...

▼ Grooming needs
Whether you have a short-haired, long-haired, or curly-haired dog, all breeds need grooming regularly to keep them looking and feeling their best.

▲ Friend for life
Choosing a new puppy or adult dog to join your family is an exciting experience, but one that comes with big responsibilities.

▲ Out and about
Regular exercise is vital for your dog's mental and physical health. Whether "free running", walking on a lead, or playing games of fetch, it is a time you can enjoy together.

The connection between an owner and dog can be a deeply rewarding relationship. Dogs have co-existed with humans for thousands of years, and today they still fulfil many important jobs – not least as loyal companions and much-loved members of our households. Dogs are dependent on us for all their needs, and as dog owners it is our job to keep our animals physically healthy and to give them the opportunity to express their natural instincts. This book will introduce you to all aspects

of essential dog care, from carrying out regular health checks to setting basic rules for training, so that you can build a happy and healthy life with your dog.

Bringing a new dog into your life requires preparation and planning. If you don't yet own a dog, this book offers guidance on choosing a puppy or adult dog that is right for your household and lifestyle, together with an overview of popular breeds and their specific training, grooming, and exercise needs. There's advice on

making your home safe and comfortable for a new dog, and on helping your pet to settle into your household including getting him used to new people and other pets, and tips on how to care for him while travelling or if you go away.

All dogs, whatever their size, age, or breed, require a certain level of daily care and attention in the form of diet, exercise, play, and grooming. Your dog needs a healthy, balanced diet to give him all the nutrients he needs. This book will show you how to tailor a diet suitable for your dog's age and activity levels, and details the foods that may be unhealthy or even harmful. Hints and tips on exercise and play, followed by guidance on grooming and bathing are included to help you give your dog the best possible care.

Basic training is fundamental to a good working relationship between you and your dog – one in which you are a gentle but effective "pack leader". The friendships that we enjoy with other people don't work with dogs. They feel most secure if they can trust us to be a firm but kind "leader". Whether you own a puppy or an older dog, this book has information on positive training methods that your dog will easily understand and accept, as well as ways to structure training sessions. There is step-by-step information on teaching basic commands such as "sit" and "stay", and training your dog to walk on a lead; as well as a look at fun, social activities such as canine sports and agility competitions.

An important part of being a good owner is keeping your dog healthy and dealing promptly with any illnesses or injuries. This book will provide you with a basic understanding of the disorders and diseases that may affect your dog at some point in his life and, most importantly, to help you recognise the warning signs of when to take him to your vet. A checklist of the signs of good health, and ill health, is included plus advice on routine checks to be done by you or your vet, and top tips on avoiding possible health problems. From serious disorders such as heart disease to minor but irritating ailments like itchy fleas, information is given on all the various health issues that can affect your dog, plus advice on how to nurse him while he recuperates.

Injuries and emergencies involving dogs can be frightening for you as well as the dog. This book covers the principles of life-saving and guides you through the initial steps needed to cope with injuries and other serious conditions, as well as giving advice on avoiding dangers such as hypothermia and heat stroke. Having an understanding of basic canine first aid will help you to feel prepared and in control, should you ever find yourself in a situation that requires it.

For a dog owner, the thought of bringing up your own puppies can be irresistible; however, breeding needs to be approached in a very careful, responsible way. Should you decide to go ahead, there is advice on the issues that you need to think about, as well as detailed information on caring for your bitch during pregnancy and whelping (giving birth), and while she is nursing her puppies. This book also has guidance on caring for your puppies in their first weeks, and helping them develop, plus tips on finding loving and secure homes for your youngsters.

Owning a dog is a commitment that comes with a great deal of responsibility, but the rewards for both of you are immense. In this book you will find all the information you need to ensure you have a well-behaved, happy, and healthy canine companion for many years to come.

1

Your new dog

Becoming a dog owner

A dog can be a fantastic, fun addition to your home – but dogs are also complex, intelligent animals and need a lot of care and attention. Owning a dog is a big responsibility.

First considerations

Before buying or adopting a dog, you need to think very carefully about what kind you want and how you plan to look after him. Keep in mind that dogs can live for up to 18 years; you need to be committed to caring for your pet over his entire lifespan.

Do you have other pets or very young children? Is anyone in your home allergic to dogs?

Find out about suitable breeds in advance (pp.14–17). Remember though that temperament is more important than looks. Could you cope with an active dog with lots of energy, or would you prefer a calm one?

to fit in with your family's routine as he grows up but at first he will need extra care and should not be left alone for long periods. So if everyone is out of the house all day, you may be better off adopting an adult dog.

Would you prefer a male or a female? Males tend to be more affectionate with people but can be easily distracted during training. Un-neutered males can also be aggressive. Females are thought to be calmer with children.

> "Dogs are not cheap pets so be sure you can afford the costs of care. They also need a lot of company, especially puppies."

First, you need to be sure that a dog is the right pet for you. Do you have the time to look after, train, and play with a puppy? Can you afford to keep a dog? Is your home environment suitable (pp.18–9)?

Do you need a dog who is good with children? Large dogs can require a lot of care and will need more food, which can be expensive, so would you be just as happy with a smaller dog?

What age is best? A puppy will learn

▲ **Grooming**
All dogs need regular grooming and baths but if you choose a long-haired breed, be aware that you may have to devote a lot of time to these tasks.

◄ **A trial run**
A good way to find out whether life as a dog owner is right for you is by offering to look after a friend's or relative's dog for a few days as a trial run.

► A family pet
If you have young children, see if you can introduce them to different breeds or types of dog to find out which ones your children prefer.

Essentials of dog care

Dogs are not cheap pets so you need to be sure you can afford the costs of care. The likely costs for your new dog include:

■ Food per week – food is a major cost, especially for large dogs.
■ Pet insurance – premiums vary considerably between providers and depend on the age and breed of dog and your home location.
■ Accessories such as collar, lead, food bowls, bed, and medications.
■ Allowance for possible extra costs such as vet's bills or a boarding kennel if you go away.

Work out how much time per day you can commit to your dog. When will you feed him? When can you

▼ Looking at dog breeds
Take the chance to watch different breeds in action at a dog show or even at an obedience class so you can get an idea of their nature as well as appearance.

exercise him – or is there someone else who can do this? All dogs need exercise and mental stimulation and some need at least an hour of exercise a day (pp.38–41). Dogs also need a lot of company, especially puppies. In addition, dogs need regular grooming and baths; long-coated dogs require extensive grooming and some breeds of dogs may require visits to a professional dog groomer.

You are responsible for your pet's welfare and in many countries, there are even laws to ensure that pet owners care for their animals properly. Essential duties include making sure that your dog has a safe place to live, good food, and plenty of company (see box, above). As a dog owner you also need to make certain that your pet will not cause harm to himself or to other people or animals.

St. Bernard

Miniature Pinscher

English Cocker Spaniel

German Shepherd

Staffordshire Bull Terrier

Beagle

Canadian Eskimo

Choosing a puppy

Puppies are delightful and will grow to fit your family but they require intensive care and training. It is best to acquire a puppy from the person who bred him if possible, and meet the pup before you take ownership.

Where to get a puppy

If you prefer to select a pure-bred puppy ask your country's Kennel Club, breed societies, or animal welfare charities for advice on good breeders in your area. If you would be happy with a cross-bred dog, you can often adopt puppies from rescue centres or even from people you might know.

It is always best to buy from the person who bred the puppy. It is unwise to buy from advertisements, as you often can't tell where a puppy comes from. Also avoid pet shops, which can be traumatic places for pups, and which may get their puppies from disreputable "puppy farms". Never buy a pup without meeting him first and never buy on impulse.

Visiting a breeder

Good breeders provide a "family" environment to give their pups the best start in life. Check that the pups live with their mother and avoid any kennels where pups are shown on their own.

Find a breeder who will allow you to spend time with the litter. Check that the puppies are being raised indoors and with plenty of human contact. Watch for any signs that they may not be used to being in a house – for example, being startled by normal domestic noises, such as a phone ringing. Look at the mother (and father if he is present). Are they friendly? Have they been screened for any inherited diseases associated with that breed? Check that the kennels look and smell clean. Is the pups' sleeping area separate from the toilet area?

The breeder may ask how much experience you have with that breed or with dogs in general, or how you intend to care for the pup. You should also have the chance to ask questions. Will the puppy be wormed and vaccinated? Will the breeder give you advice for the first few weeks after you have bought your pup, or let you return it if things don't work out?

▲ **Mother and puppies**
Young pups should live with their mother and siblings. The breeder should let you meet the mother and see the whole litter together.

> "Never buy a pup without meeting him first and never buy on impulse. And never because you feel sorry for him!"

Owner's checklist from breeder

■ Print-out of pedigree.
■ Breed registration papers.
■ Certificate of inoculations.
■ Worming history documentation.
■ Printed declaration that the pup is healthy and has a good body structure, and that these factors will be verified by your own vet.
■ A diet sheet giving food and feeding regime with a sample of the puppy's current food.

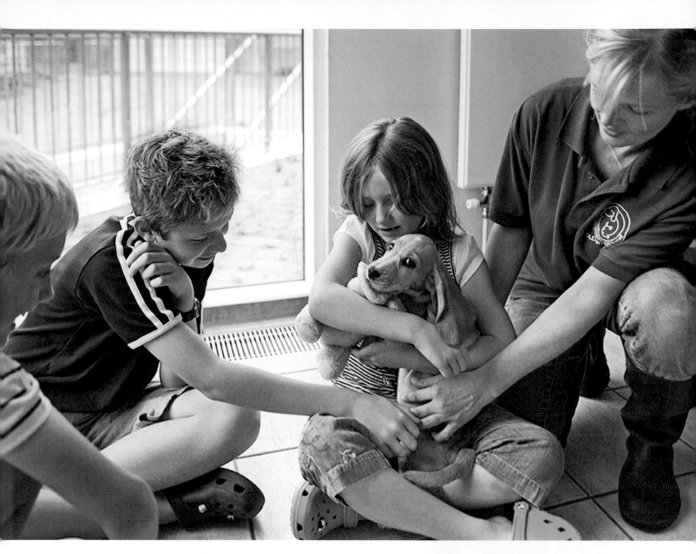

▲ Family decision
Choosing a puppy is an exciting, emotional experience for children. Select a likely candidate before your children meet the pup to ensure a happy outcome.

► Rescue pup
Rescue centres occasionally offer puppies who have been abandoned, orphaned, or whose owner has had to give them up. Since the pups have had a difficult start in life they may need special care.

Don't forget to collect all necessary information from the breeder (see box, left).

Selecting your puppy

A puppy should enjoy meeting you and being handled. A pup that snaps at you could have a dominant personality and be hard to train, while one that hides from you may need a lot of patience to ensure it does not grow into a nervous adult. Never pick a puppy because you feel sorry for it!

Look out for any signs of ill health, such as runny eyes or nose, diarrhoea, thin or pot-bellied body, dull fur, or scabby patches.

If you have children, visit the puppies yourself first, then take the children once you have made an initial choice.

Choosing an adult dog

Although puppies are cute and appealing, you may find that an older dog, which does not need as much training, suits your lifestyle better. You can obtain an adult dog from a rescue centre or even from someone you know.

Rescue centres

A common way to acquire an adult dog is from a rescue centre. Some rescue shelters are run by welfare charities and rehome dogs of many sizes and ages. Others specialize in particular dog breeds that have re-homing issues such as greyhounds after the end of their racing career, or dogs with specific care and training needs such as Dobermanns and Staffordshire Bull Terriers. Some breed societies run a breed rescue service and these can be accessed through breed society websites (see p.163 for contact details).

An adult dog will take time to get used to you; however, he may already have been house-trained and socialized. At a rescue centre, the dogs' temperaments will have been assessed so you will know if they need a town or country home, are friendly with other pets and children, and whether or not they need to live with a companion. Whether a pure-bred or cross-bred dog, it is wisest to base your selection on temperament more than looks. Spending time at a rescue centre may tell you a lot about the dog's predominant traits.

◄ **Rescue dog**
All dogs need a loving home but dogs from rescue centres may need particular care and patience from their owners. Get to know a new dog first before deciding if he suits you.

> "An adult dog will take time to get used to you but he may already have been socialized."

Having an assessment

Many of the dogs at rescue centres will have had difficult experiences such as separation from previous owners or even neglect or abuse, so staff will be keen to see that they go to a loving and protective home. You may have to fill in an application form, attend an interview at the centre (perhaps with other family members), and have your home inspected by rescue centre staff before being allowed to adopt a pet.

In return, you will have the opportunity to ask questions and meet suitable dogs. The dog may already be neutered and microchipped, and may have a veterinary examination before being handed over to you. You may have to pay an adoption fee, which might cover benefits such as a "starter pack" of food, advice on care and behavioural issues, and help with matters such as pet insurance and guidance on the ongoing cost of owning a dog.

◄ **Family interview**
Rescue centre staff will want to interview all members of your family and find out about your home and daily life so they can decide which dogs will best match your lifestyle.

Choosing a dog breed

Whether you already have a favourite breed in mind or are still trying to decide, the information in this section will help you work out which dogs would fit best with your lifestyle and preferences.

Breed groups

There are hundreds of dog breeds in the world and international organizations classify breeds based on their traditional or current uses. Although a dog's character is most strongly formed by its environment and upbringing, looking at breeds by group can give you a general idea of their needs.

■ Working dogs – this group includes guard and herding dogs. They are easy to train but need plenty of physical and mental activity to keep them happy.

■ Spitz-type dogs – originally used for work in Arctic regions, these dogs are highly energetic.

■ Sight hounds – these athletic, independent dogs have a strong chasing instinct which needs to be controlled and given an outlet.

■ Scent hounds – many hunting dogs tend to be pack animals and are family-friendly. These dogs need plenty of chances to nose around outdoors.

■ Terriers – bred to tackle small animals, these compact dogs have a feisty nature and a strong digging instinct, which can become destructive if the dog is bored.

■ Gundogs – these friendly hunting dogs are good family pets. Their liking for wet, muddy places can lead to extra grooming needs.

■ Companion dogs – bred mainly for domestic or decorative purposes, most of these breeds are small and easy to keep.

Using the charts

When choosing a breed, consider your lifestyle and home environment – large dogs need plenty of space, and some breeds take longer to train than others. Some dogs need weekly grooming (low), while others need it 2–3 times weekly (medium), or daily brushing (high). Exercise needs also vary from as little as 30 minutes a day (low), 1–2 hours a day (medium), to more than 2 hours a day (high).

WORKING							
	German Shepherd	Border Collie	Pembroke Welsh Corgi	Rottweiler	Shar Pei	Boxer	Great Dane
SIZE	Large	Medium	Small	Medium	Medium	Medium	Large
EXERCISE	High	High	Medium	High	Medium	High	High
GROOMING	Medium	Medium	Low	Low	Low	Low	Low
TRAINABILITY	Easy	Easy	Quite easy	Quite easy	Quite easy	Quite easy	Quite easy

SPITZ-TYPE

	Siberian Husky	Samoyed	Norwegian Elkhound	Akita	Chow Chow	Japanese Spitz	Pomeranian
SIZE	Medium	Medium	Large	Large	Medium	Small	Small
EXERCISE	High	High	Medium	High	Medium	Medium	Low
GROOMING	Medium	High	Medium	Low	High	High	Low
TRAINABILITY	Quite easy	Quite easy	Quite easy	Quite easy	Quite easy	Quite easy	Quite easy

SIGHT HOUNDS

	Greyhound	Italian Greyhound	Whippet	Borzoi	Saluki	Irish Wolfhound	Afghan Hound
SIZE	Large	Small	Medium	Large	Large	Large	Large
EXERCISE	Medium	Medium	Medium	Medium	High	High	High
GROOMING	Low	Medium	Low	Medium	Low	Medium	High
TRAINABILITY	Quite easy	Quite easy	Quite easy	Not so easy	Quite easy	Easy	Not so easy

SCENT HOUNDS

	Bloodhound	Otterhound	Petit Basset Griffon Vendeen	Beagle	Dachshund (long-hair)	Dobermann	Rhodesian Ridgeback
SIZE	Medium	Medium	Small	Small	Small	Large	Medium
EXERCISE	High	High	High	High	Medium	High	High
GROOMING	Low	Medium	Medium	Low	Medium	Low	Low
TRAINABILITY	Quite easy	Quite easy	Quite easy	Quite easy	Quite easy	Quite easy	Quite easy

TERRIERS

	West Highland White Terrier	Yorkshire Terrier	Jack Russell	Airedale Terrier	Border Terrier	Staffordshire Bull Terrier	Miniature Schnauzer
SIZE	Small	Small	Small	Medium	Small	Small	Medium
EXERCISE	Medium	Low	Medium	Medium	Medium	Medium	Medium
GROOMING	Medium	High	Low	Medium	Medium	Low	High
TRAINABILITY	Easy	Quite easy	Quite easy	Quite easy	Quite easy	Quite easy	Easy

GUNDOGS

	English Cocker Spaniel	Portuguese Water Dog	Irish Setter	German Pointer	Weimaraner	Labrador Retriever	Curly Coated Retriever
SIZE	Medium	Medium	Large	Medium	Large	Medium	Large
EXERCISE	Medium	Medium	High	High	High	High	High
GROOMING	High	High	Medium	Low	Low	Low	Medium
TRAINABILITY	Quite easy	Easy	Quite easy	Easy	Easy	Easy	Easy

COMPANION

	Pekingese	Shih Tzu	Miniature Poodle	Cavalier King Charles Spaniel	Chinese Crested	Chihuahua	Dalmatian
SIZE	Small	Small	Small	Small	Small	Small	Large
EXERCISE	Low	Medium	Medium	Medium	Low	Low	High
GROOMING	High	High	High	Medium	Low	Medium	Low
TRAINABILITY	Not so easy	Easy	Easy	Quite easy	Quite easy	Easy	Quite easy

The dog-proof home

Before you collect your new dog, check your home and garden for anything that may cause him harm and remove or put them out of reach to ensure a safe environment for your new pet.

Danger areas

The best prevention is to keep a close eye on your dog. Otherwise, to spot potential dangers you need to get down to dog level and do a thorough check for the following possible hazards:

■ Escape routes – a dog can dart through doors, under gates, or down stairs and run into the street.

■ Confined spaces – dogs can squeeze into gaps such as behind a fridge and get stuck.

■ Poisons – dogs love to eat so this is a big risk. Look out for poisonous plants (animal welfare societies often have lists), toxic chemicals, and even harmful human foods such as chocolates and grapes or raisins (pp.142–3).

■ Things to chew and swallow – flexes can cause electrical injuries; sharp objects can hurt a dog's gullet; items such as balloons can cause blockages lower down.

■ Heavy or sharp things – items such as razor blades in the bathroom or garden tools in the shed can cause injuries.

■ Slick floor surfaces – tiles or lino can be slippery if they (or the dog) are wet.

Outdoor checklist

■ Close off any gaps in hedges or fencing or under gates.
■ Move or get rid of toxic plants.
■ Make sure your dog will have shade in the garden.
■ Keep garage or shed doors shut to keep your dog away from machinery, sharp or heavy tools, or chemicals such as antifreeze, paints, and paint thinner.
■ Keep poisons and fertilizers locked up or on a high shelf.
■ Keep your dog away from areas where poisons or slug pellets have been used; dispose of dead animals that have eaten poison.
■ Never leave your dog alone with a barbecue – hot coals and sharp kebab sticks can cause injury.

DON'T...
leave a barbecue unattended if you are cooking food.

DO...
keep rubbish bins covered and chemicals locked up.

DON'T...
let your dog roam freely except in fenced-in areas, and make sure you close up any holes in fences so he cannot escape.

DO...
use a bin with a secure lid so your dog cannot raid it.

DON'T...
leave things lying around that your dog could chew.

Indoor checklist

■ Keep hard floors dry, and towel-dry a wet dog promptly.
■ Keep outside doors shut; fit a stair gate.
■ Block any small gaps behind or between furniture.
■ Fix frayed electrical cords.
■ Fit child locks to cabinet doors and drawers.
■ Use dustbins with secure lids.
■ Put cleaning chemicals away.
■ Keep medicines in the cabinet.
■ Get rid of any toxic houseplants.
■ Check floors and low surfaces for small or sharp items.
■ At festival times, keep your dog away from fragile decorations and lit candles. Find a safe place for him to hide from fireworks.

DO...
put your puppy in a playpen when you are busy. Make sure it contains a bed, toys or chews, newspaper, and a water bowl.

DO...
make sure the gate is fastened and low enough to the ground to keep a puppy from escaping.

"The best prevention is to keep a close eye on your dog."

DO...
check for potentially poisonous plants.

Essential equipment

To ensure that you are ready for life with your new dog, it is best to obtain essential equipment in advance. You can always add extra items once your dog has arrived in your home.

Preparing for arrival

You need to obtain a bed and bowls for your dog before anything else. His bed needs to be big enough for him to stretch out and turn around in. A bed improvised from a strong cardboard box may be fine for a pup as it can be thrown away if soiled or chewed, or as the dog grows.

Moulded plastic beds are easy to clean and can withstand chewing. For both types, add a soft lining of towels or blankets. Foam beds are comfortable and many have machine-washable covers. They are good for elderly dogs with joint issues but not so suitable for dogs likely to chew or soil the bed.

Your dog will need one bowl for food and one for water. Both will need to be cleaned every day; food bowls should be cleaned before each meal. Ceramic bowls are sturdy enough even for large dogs; however, they are often straight-sided, with hard-to-reach corners. Stainless-steel bowls are easy to use and keep clean. The best are non-tip with a

> "Make your dog's bed cosy and inviting. For a new puppy, or a dog who needs extra security, use a dog crate."

◄ **Dog bed**
Beds are usually made with high sides for security and a low front so the dog can easily get in and out. Choose a warm, thick lining so that your dog is comfortable.

Dog toys

Toys enable a dog to express natural behaviour such as chasing and chewing. You can buy special dog toys like the ones shown here, or improvise your own using items such as an old football or a length of rope. Choose toys made from a substance that will not splinter or choke your dog, and are large enough not to get stuck in the dog's throat.
To prevent bad habits, do not use old clothes or shoes.

Rubber chew toy

Food-hiding toy

Dumbbells for carrying

Cuddly toy for puppy

Rope for tugging

Bowls should be stable enough to stay still during use and shaped so your dog can easily reach into the bottom and around the edges. Ceramic or stainless steel are good choices.

Ceramic bowl

Stainless-steel bowl

▲ **Puppy crate**
Put the crate in a warm, draught-free area where your puppy can see you and other members of the family during the day. It should be large enough for him to move around in.

rubber rim around the base to keep them still during use. Plastic bowls may be sufficient for puppies and smaller dogs.

You also need to take out pet insurance before taking ownership of a dog. Insurance is essential for illnesses and injuries, and covers costs if your pet is lost or dies, or if he harms a person, other animals, or property.

Home safety

You need to check that your home is safe for your dog (pp.18–19). For a new puppy or a dog who needs extra security, it can help to use a dog crate – a large pen with wire sides and top and a solid base. Line the base with newspapers in case of accidents and add bedding and toys. A crate must be a comforting "den" for your puppy. It is a good place to keep him until he is

toilet-trained, for short periods if left alone, or as a safe space if he is hurt or ill. Never leave him in the crate for long periods, or lock him inside as a punishment.

Grooming and hygiene

You will need a basic grooming kit (pp.42–3) even for short-haired dogs including a bristle-haired brush or a rubber-toothed mitt. Dogs with long or thick coats may need a long-bristled brush, round-ended scissors for trimming hair, and de-tangling spray; your vet or a breed society can guide you. You will also need shampoo and a towel for bathing your dog, and perhaps nail clippers.

For clearing up dog faeces outdoors, carry small biodegradable bags. Vets and pet shops sell bags specially for this purpose.

Collars and leads

Use a soft fabric collar for a pup, fastened so that you can slip two fingers between it and the pup's neck, and check every week that it is not getting too tight. For adult dogs use fabric or leather collars, or a harness for a strong dog. Avoid metal choke chains. Attach a name tag to your dog's collar, giving your contact details.

Name tag

Collar

Lead

Bringing your dog home

Introducing a new pet into your home will be exciting but perhaps a bit nerve-racking – not least for your dog. Prepare as much as possible beforehand and plan for the first day at home to be quiet and calm.

Being prepared

Make sure your home is "dog-proofed" (pp.18–19) and that you have bowls and bedding ready for when the dog arrives (pp.20–21). Have at least a week's supply of food and collect any diet sheets and initial supplies from the breeder or animal shelter.

Select a "den" area for the dog during the day – somewhere warm and quiet but where your pet can see and hear people so he will not be lonely. Place your puppy crate in this area if you are using one (p.21). Have newspapers ready to put on the floor in case of accidents.

If you are getting a young puppy,

> "Introduce your dog to your home slowly so that he can get used to his new environment."

letting the pup sleep in a box or basket in your bedroom can help him to settle in. You need to have a name ready. Choose a name of one or two syllables as this will be easy for the dog to learn, but avoid any names that could be confused with words you might use to command the dog such as "stay" or "no".

Arriving home

As soon as you get home with your dog or puppy, take him into the garden as he may wish to relieve himself. Then let your dog into your

▲ **Let him explore**
Your dog might like to sniff scents and look around the garden. Allow him to do so as it will help him relax and habituate better to your home and the new surroundings.

house and let him explore. For the first day at least, keep your pet in his den area so he can get used to the home slowly. A puppy will probably tire quite quickly so allow him to sleep whenever he wants.

Meeting family members

Introduce your dog to everyone in the family. If you have children, supervise them for the first few days as they and the dog get used to each other. Explain to the children in advance that your new dog may be feeling a bit nervous so they need to

▲ **Settling down**
For the first few nights, your puppy may feel more secure if he is sleeping in a box in the bedroom. Speak to him gently if he whimpers but don't make a fuss of him.

be quiet around him. To meet the dog, have the children come into the room with him and sit down quietly and give them treats to offer him. Say that they need to let the dog come to them of his own accord. Explain that the dog will enjoy playing with them but they have to keep play sessions short for the first few days so he does not get tired or over-excited. They must not grab the dog or pick him up suddenly as he could get frightened and bite them.

Meeting other pets

Let your new dog meet other pets one at a time after the first day or so, once he has settled in.

Introduce resident dogs to the new one in "neutral territory" such as the garden so there is room to escape if one of them gets nervous. Make a fuss

of your resident dog before paying attention to the new one to reduce any risk of jealousy.

To introduce a cat, choose a large room or the garden and hold on to the dog while the cat comes to meet him. Make sure the cat has an easy escape route in case the dog gets too boisterous. Never feed cats and dogs together as the dog may try to steal the cat's food. If you have rabbits or other small animals, keep them in a hutch and supervise the dog whenever he is around them.

The first few days

Take things quietly for the first few days to let your dog settle in and get to know his new home. Make sure there is always at least one member of the family around to keep an eye on him.

Getting into a routine

Establish a routine from day one – feed your dog and take him outside to relieve himself at regular times. Set the ground rules for what your dog is allowed to do and where he is allowed to go. For example, if you don't want your dog to go upstairs or lie on chairs or beds, teach him this rule right from the outset.

Getting used to the home

Introduce your dog to any noisy or potentially frightening household machines such as the vacuum cleaner and washing machine. Let him be

▲ **Getting confident**
For a puppy, a new home can be quite a scary place. Get him used to noisy appliances like the vacuum cleaner so that as he grows he becomes confident in the human world.

◄ **A regular routine**
Take your puppy or dog outside to relieve himself at regular times – whatever the weather. A set routine will help him to avoid having accidents in the house.

> "Establish a routine from day one – feed your dog and take him outside to relieve himself at regular times. Set the ground rules for what he can do."

▲ Keeping your dog entertained
If you have to leave your dog alone in the house, leave a toy with him to keep him entertained and occupied while you are gone.

▶ Separation training
Start by leaving your dog for a couple of minutes at a time, a few times a day, and gradually extend this as he accepts being alone.

present while the machine is running but at a comfortable distance with an "escape route" if he needs it. If your dog looks nervous, get down to his level and speak to him in a gentle, encouraging tone, or distract him with a toy, until he seems calmer.

House-training

Dogs instinctively avoid soiling their "nest" area, and this is a useful basis for toilet training. Bear in mind that there may be a few accidents in the house before your puppy is fully trained.

Developing a routine will help avoid accidents. Take your pup outside after eating, when he first wakes up after a nap, just before bedtime, and just after any exciting event (such as meeting a new person). You may need to take a young pup out about once an hour. Keep to his toileting times as closely as possible. Watch for signs that your pup needs to "go" such as

sniffing the ground, turning in circles, and squatting. If you notice any of these, take him out immediately. Stay outdoors with your dog until he relieves himself. As soon as he does so, give him lots of praise.

Home alone

Being alone is stressful for dogs; if they are not trained to tolerate this, they can become destructive or noisy, or may have accidents in the house. Your dog needs to learn that he will be safe on his own and trust that you will return.

To begin training, choose a time when the dog is calm or even sleepy. Start by leaving him in his pen or a room for just a few minutes. When you come back in, don't make a fuss of him; just stay nearby quietly until he calms down. Extend the periods gradually until he can be left for several hours without becoming stressed.

When you go out and leave your dog at home, make sure he has access to his bed and a bowl of water. Also give him a toy with food hidden in it to keep him occupied for a while after you have left.

Socializing your dog

Your puppy will need to get used to people, cars, and the outside world. Training may also be necessary for an older dog who lacks confidence or has behavioural problems outside the home.

Local walks

Once your puppy has been inoculated and microchipped he can be taken for walks. It is important to expose young pups to as many different situations as possible. Once puppies reach 12 weeks, their attitude becomes more guarded and if they encounter something strange their first instinct will be to run away.

▼ New faces
Walks are a great way for your dog to meet people that he may not normally see, such as toddlers and teenagers. You can use toys and treats to make these encounters more fun.

For older dogs, walks are about letting them get to know their "territory". Even so, there may be things that your dog has not encountered before such as livestock and wild animals.

Creating confidence

When your dog first ventures into the wider world, the experience can be overwhelming for him. Some things may be frightening such as cars and lorries. Others may be powerful distractions: for example, a toddler on a tricycle or lambs in a field could trigger your dog's

chasing instinct. Your dog needs to learn confidence – and you need to be sure you can depend on him to behave in all situations.

Introduce your pet to anyone who wants to meet him. If you have children, meet them from school with your pup so he gets used to seeing other children.

When acquainting your dog with other dogs, start with those you already know. You could arrange "puppy play dates" at home or go out for walks with someone who has an older, easy-going dog. If your dog is upset by strange dogs, walk away

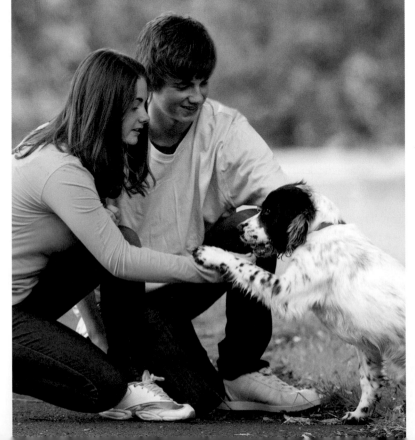

Getting used to traffic

- Introduce your dog to startling or distracting sights such as noisy cars by getting him to sit at a comfortable distance while the vehicle goes by.
- Crouch down and hold him so he does not try to chase, and praise him when he sits quietly.
- Reward him with a treat once the object has passed.
- Gradually get him used to being closer to these objects but at a safe distance from fast traffic.
- Be patient – let him take his time.

▲ Meeting livestock
It is best to view cows, sheep, horses, and other livestock through a fence or gate rather than going into the field with them. Use a lead to prevent your dog from possibly giving chase.

► Comfortable journeys
Make sure your dog has space to lie down and turn around comfortably in a car. If using a dog guard, your dog can be left free in the back. Use a blanket or pillows to make him comfortable.

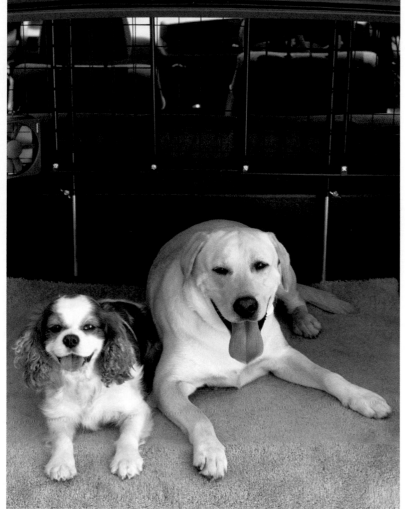

from them or ask the owners to hold their dogs or put them on the lead while you pass.

It is best to keep your dog on a lead around livestock and wild animals – even for a quiet dog, the temptation to chase can be sudden and irresistible. In many countries, dog owners have a legal duty to prevent their animals from harassing livestock.

Get your dog used to distractions such as motor vehicles, bicycles, prams, and people on roller-skates or skateboards (see box, left).

Travelling by car

As a dog owner you have a legal duty to transport your dog in a way that keeps the dog and other vehicle occupants safe. If you have a large car, you could fit a dog guard behind the rear seats; this should be sufficient for short journeys under one hour. For long trips or in a larger vehicle put your dog in a dog crate. If your dog is travelling on the back seat of your car, a dog harness that links in with the seat belt system can restrain him safely.

Start travel training by teaching your dog to sit in the car for a few minutes with the engine off and the doors open. Graduate to sitting in the car with the doors closed and engine on for a few minutes. Then start taking short journeys of a few minutes, building up to longer trips.

When travelling, don't let your dog stick his head out of the window as he could risk head or eye injuries. For long journeys, carry water and a bowl and stop at least every two hours for your dog to have a drink and to get out and relieve himself. Switch on the air conditioning if your car has it, and never leave your dog alone inside a car even with the windows ajar – on a warm day or in direct sunlight, heat stroke can kill a dog in as little as 20 minutes (pp.146-7). Watch for any signs of travel sickness such as drooling or panting. Excessive barking or chewing on the car's interiors are other signs of distress. To help prevent these, make sure your dog has a non-slip surface to stand on in the car.

Going on holiday

Nowadays there is an increasing number of "dog-friendly" holidays available for you and your pet. If you do need to leave your dog though, there are also options to ensure he is well cared for while you are away.

Travelling together

Travelling with your dog can be fun – with a bit of prior organization. Your dog needs to be controllable in public places and trained for car travel (p.27). He also needs to be microchipped and wear an ID tag.

If you plan to travel abroad with your dog, find out what regulations apply to taking dogs into that country and if there are any legal rules regarding car travel with dogs; animal welfare organizations may have information on these issues. You may need to have your dog vaccinated for diseases such as rabies. Also arrange travel insurance for him. Find out how the airline or ferry company usually transports dogs. Ferry companies may provide open-air kennels on deck or air-conditioned spaces inside the vessel. Airlines may require your dog to travel in a special crate and they also have transport rules for dogs. Check in advance that your destination will be dog-friendly.

Take a good supply of your dog's usual food, and familiar items such as food bowls. Keep to your routine of feeding, walks, and bedtimes as much as possible to minimize stress.

▲ Comfortable car journey
Your dog should have enough space to move and stretch during a car journey, especially if the journey is likely to be several hours.

▶ Meeting a pet sitter
If you decide to leave your dog at home, introduce him to any potential sitter so that you can assess how well the sitter gets on with him.

▼ Family kennels
If you have two dogs, check with the boarding kennels that they have a kennel big enough to house both dogs together. It will reassure your dogs to stay together and help them settle into the new environment.

▲ Exercising safely
Some dogs are not fond of other dogs. Let your sitter or kennels know if your dog will accept being exercised with other dogs, and whether he is particularly shy or strong-willed, which could affect how he gets on with strange dogs.

Leaving your dog behind

If you do not plan to take your dog with you, there are several ways to arrange care while you are away. Whichever option you choose, you need to be sure your dog is used to being separated from you (p.25).

You could ask a relative, friend, or neighbour to "pet sit", or employ a registered pet sitter. It is advisable to leave your dog with this person rather than alone in your home. If you can, arrange a few visits to the pet sitter's home in advance so that it becomes a familiar place to your dog. Make sure your dog will be wearing an ID tag at all times. Leave a good supply of his food with the sitter, plus notes on feeding, walking, and bedtimes, and emergency contact numbers for you and for the vet. If you plan to use a registered sitter, ask your vet or fellow dog owners for suggestions on suitable people, and ask the sitter for references.

Another option is to use boarding kennels. Your vet or other local dog owners should be able to recommend good ones. Staying in kennels can be more stressful for your dog than staying in a home environment. It is wise to visit the kennels before using them to see whether they will be suitable (see box, right). Remember to book well in advance, especially at busy times of the year and if the kennel is a popular one.

"When travelling abroad, check in advance that your destination is dog-friendly."

Boarding kennels

When assessing kennels, you need to check that they have the following:

■ Licence from a local authority.
■ Environment – the kennels and common areas should be clean, warm, draught-free, and secure. Each kennel should have a raised platform that your dog can lie on or under.
■ Feeding – staff should keep to your dog's usual foods and feeding times.
■ Handling and exercise – dogs should get attention and exercise at least twice a day.
■ Veterinary care – access to 24-hour care.

2

Everyday care

A balanced diet

Dogs need more than just meat – they need a healthy, balanced diet and the right quantity for their size. Most people buy ready-prepared dog food but you could make your own if you prefer.

Essential elements

A good diet should provide all of the nutrients that a dog needs and must contain these elements:

■ Proteins – the "building blocks" of cells, proteins help to build muscles and repair the body. Lean meat, eggs, and dairy products are good sources of proteins.

■ Fats – high in energy and making food more tasty, fats also contain essential fatty acids, which help to maintain cell walls and aid growth and wound healing in your dog. They are the source of vitamins A, D, E, and K, and are found in meat, oily fish, and in oils such as linseed oil and sunflower oil.

■ Fibre – found in potatoes, vegetables, and rice, fibre helps to bulk out food and slow your dog's digestion, allowing more time to absorb nutrients and making it easier for him to pass faeces.

■ Vitamins and minerals – these help to maintain your dog's body structures such as skin, bones, and blood cells, and support the chemical reactions that turn food into energy or enable vital body functions such as blood clotting.

■ Water – as with humans, water is essential for your dog's life. Make sure your dog has access to fresh water. Refill the bowl with water two or three times a day.

Commercial foods

These foods can be moist, semi-moist, or dry. Dry foods can help keep teeth and gums healthy but check that they have wholesome core ingredients. You must provide plenty of water too, as dogs who are fed dried food drink more. Moist foods have a lot of moisture content along with higher fat and protein components.

The advantages of commercial foods include a wide choice of brands; foods made for specific groups such as

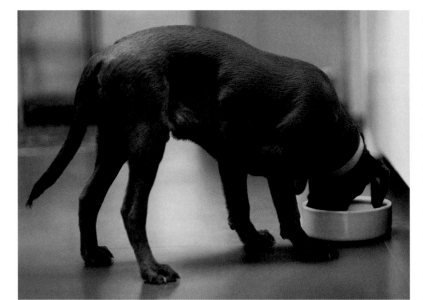

◄ Healthy diet
Your dog's energy level, his life span, general wellbeing, and behaviour all depend on the type of food he eats.

► Varieties of food
The choice of foods available for dogs has greatly expanded. This ranges from specially developed commercial foods – moist, dry, or semi-moist – to natural foods that can be prepared at home.

Moist food

Dry food

Natural food

Give a dog a bone?

Vets tend to advise against feeding bones as they can cause blockages in the digestive system. Never feed cooked bones as these can splinter and injure your dog's mouth or gullet. Instead, choose bone-type treats or chews made of hide, which can keep his teeth healthy and satisfy the urge to chew but without the risks of real bones.

Sterilized bone

Rawhide chews

▲ A good choice
Rawhide chews are a safer alternative to real bones. They are also useful to help occupy your dog when he is left alone for periods at home.

puppies, seniors, and pregnant or lactating bitches; clearly defined nutritional values; and ease of use. However, these foods can contain ingredients such as preservatives and flavourings that could disagree with your dog. Check the labels on these items if you are unsure of the ingredients, and look at the websites of pet food standards organizations for guidance.

Natural foods

Instead of feeding your dog a packaged diet, you can prepare a home-made natural diet in the form of raw meat. You will also need to add cooked vegetables and starchy foods such as rice to provide fibre, and check with your vet if you need to add a vitamin and mineral supplement.

This diet is closer to how a dog might eat in the wild, and you know there are no preservatives or other hidden extras. However, natural foods need to be carefully balanced and it can be difficult to ensure consistent

nutritional quality or to adapt the diet to different energy needs of dogs. Preparation of fresh food on a daily basis can also take a lot of time.

Treats and chews

Many dog owners give extra-tasty foods when training or simply as a treat. Some treats can be high in fats so if you give them to your pet regularly, make sure to reduce his main meals to prevent overeating. You can buy treats at pet shops or make the treats at home. Dogs prefer smelly and soft treats that have more meat in them, so try giving your dog treats with foods such as cheese and chicken or sausages in them.

► Dog treats
There are many different types of tasty treats you can give your dog, and they are useful rewards for good behaviour. Try out different treats to see which one he likes best. Only allow your dog a few treats each day though to avoid over feeding.

Chews, on the other hand, help keep your dog busy, preventing him from chewing household items such as shoes and furniture or biting your hands. Chews are especially good for puppies during teething. They also play an important role in keeping your dog's teeth clean and help keep his jaws in good condition.

> "A natural diet is closer to how a dog might eat in the wild."

Cooked sausage

Cheese cubes

Moist treats

Meaty treats

Bite-sized treats

Monitoring feeding levels

As with humans, animals can develop health problems due to overeating or a poor diet. Make sure your dog eats the right amount of food to maintain an optimal weight for his breed or size.

Good feeding habits

The way you feed your dog is as important as what you feed him:

■ Set regular meal times.

■ Make sure you wash the feed bowls before every use.

■ Clear away feed bowls when your dog has finished eating, especially if feeding moist canned or home-made foods.

■ Don't feed your dog the same things that you eat – his needs are different, and some foods for humans, such as chocolate, can be poisonous to dogs (pp.142–3).

■ If you need to alter your dog's diet, make changes gradually to avoid any stomach upset.

■ Check that fresh drinking water is available at all times.

> "Do not feed your dog scraps from the table, and never give in to begging for food."

Eating too fast?

It is natural for a dog to eat fast; in the wild, this would stop other pack members stealing his food. If your dog gobbles his food too quickly, try using an anti-gorge bowl. This has lumpy protrusions in the base that your dog has to work around as he eats, thus slowing his rate of eating. This can help prevent digestive problems such as wind, vomiting, and indigestion.

Preventing obesity

Some dog breeds are prone to put on weight, such as the Basset Hound, Cavalier King Charles, Dachshund, and Labrador. However, any dog can get fat with too much high-energy food and too little exercise. Over feeding your dog can lead to heart problems, diabetes, and painful joints. In particular, for breeds that have large bodies and thin legs (such as the Rottweiler or the Staffordshire Bull Terrier), weight coupled with exercise can cause ligament problems. To prevent weight problems in your dog:

■ Feed for your dog's age, size, and

Lumpy protrusions

▲ **Anti-gorge bowl**
The anti-gorge bowl does not allow dogs to take large bites of food as they must eat around the moulded shapes. This results in a slower, more relaxed feeding time.

activity level (pp.36–7).

■ Be extra vigilant about feeding treats to your dog; don't feed scraps from the table, and never give in to begging for food.

■ Ask your vet about a balanced diet for weight loss.

■ Weigh smaller dogs at home on bathroom scales. If your dog is large, ask your vet's surgery if he can be weighed there.

■ Keep an eye on your dog's body shape – this can be just as helpful as weighing him. You can even take photos every week to monitor any changes in his weight.

A healthy weight

You need to check your dog's condition regularly to ensure that he is not too fat or too thin. Body shapes differ between breeds, so find out what is normal for your dog's breed. If you are not sure about the right quantity to feed, ask your vet.

▲ **Thin**
The face looks thin, the ribs easily felt or seen, and the tummy more drawn in than normal for the breed.

▲ **Healthy**
The fur is shiny, the body is well-muscled but not bony, and there's a slight waist.

▲ **Fat**
The tummy is large, there are rolls of fat at the back of the neck, and a thick layer of fat over the ribs.

The right portion
Always feed a balanced diet to your dog, consisting of carbohydrates, proteins, and fats. Research the correct meal size for your dog's size, age, and activity level.

Dietary change through life

Dogs at different stages of life have particular nutritional needs – whether growing puppies, nursing mothers, sport dogs, or older pets. It is important to ensure your dog has the right nutrients for health and energy for his age.

Puppies

Once puppies are weaned, they need to be fed little and often – four times a day at first, going down to three times a day from about six months. Puppies grow fast so they need high-energy food; ask your vet if you are unsure of the right quantity to feed your pup based on his size. Increase the amount slowly as he grows but avoid over feeding as this can lead to obesity in later life. It may be best to feed commercial puppy food to make sure your pup gets the right balance of nutrients.

If you have bought your puppy from a breeder, he may supply a sample of the food that the pup has been eating. Stick to this food in the beginning and introduce changes gradually.

Adult pets

For many dogs, two meals a day (morning and evening) is enough. Neutered dogs need fewer calories than un-neutered ("entire") dogs; otherwise, feed according to your dog's size and activity level. Monitor your dog's weight regularly to make sure you are giving him the right amount of food.

Working dogs

Working or sport dogs should have high-protein, energy-dense, easily digestible foods to maximize their strength, speed, and stamina. However, the volume of food given to a working dog should be no more than for a normal adult dog. Different types of work need different energy sources:
- For short, sharp bursts such as racing or agility shows, dogs need a moderately increased fat intake.
- For endurance work such as sledding, hunting, or herding animals, dogs need high fat foods with extra protein.

▲ Growing up
Always provide your puppy with a well-balanced diet to build a strong body. Be sure to choose food that is specially formulated for puppies and change to an adult formula as your puppy matures.

► Fit for the job
Working dogs such as the Collie, which are bred for their strength and stamina, require a diet rich in proteins and fat to keep them energetic while they carry out endurance work.

▲ **Nursing needs**
The nutritional requirements of a nursing mother are even more than that of a growing dog. Her calorie needs will steadily increase as the puppies grow and she produces more milk to feed them.

"For many dogs, two meals a day is enough. Feed according to size and activity level."

Nursing mothers

A pregnant bitch can stay on her usual diet until the last two to three weeks of pregnancy; from this point until whelping, her energy needs will increase by 25–50 per cent. The bitch may lose her appetite as the time to give birth approaches – this is normal. Her appetite will soon return after the puppies are born. A bitch producing milk will need two to three times as many calories than normal in the first four weeks, as the puppies' milk needs are at their highest. Feed her energy-dense food such as puppy food or working-dog food, and feed little and often. By the time the puppies begin weaning (six to eight weeks), the bitch will still need extra calories until she has stopped producing milk altogether.

Convalescent dogs

A sick dog will need easily digestible food such as boiled chicken and rice; your vet can help give you guidance. Some companies make extra-nutritious, palatable food for convalescent dogs. Feed your dog little and often and ensure the food is at body temperature so it will be more tempting. Keep a note of how much your dog is eating, and report any loss of appetite to the vet.

Older dogs

From about age seven onwards, dogs start to need more nutrients but fewer calories. Many do well on a normal adult diet, slightly reduced in quantity and with vitamin and mineral supplements (ask your vet about these). Some dog food companies produce "senior" formulas that are softer, palatable, and with higher protein, lower fat, and extra vitamins and minerals. You may need to adjust feeding to three times a day. A slower metabolic rate makes older dogs more prone to obesity. Keeping a healthy weight can improve the quality and length of your dog's life.

Fighting fit

All dogs need exercise or they can become bored and frustrated. Regular sessions daily will help your dog burn off excess energy and also help him to stay calmer at home and accept periods of being left alone.

Daily exercise

Dogs need at least two exercise sessions per day. For puppies regular exercise can help to build strength and reinforce learning, while for older dogs gentle activity can help to prevent problems such as obesity and painful joints. Dogs bred for hunting and working have higher energy levels than other breeds (see breed table on pp.14-17); two half-hour walks might be plenty for a Yorkshire Terrier or a Pug, but a Dalmatian or Boxer might need an hour-long walk or run plus a training or play session.

If your dog is under exercised, he can develop behavioural problems – he may become hyperactive and agitated and find it difficult to settle. He may also find alternative, destructive outlets for his mental and physical energies such as chewing up household furniture, barking excessively, or running away to look for entertainment.

Exercising your dog can be built into your daily activities: for example, taking the dog with you when you collect your children from school or walking him to the local shop. You could also find open areas where your dog can play or explore, or set up an exercise space in your garden. The following tips will help to keep him comfortable when exercising:

■ Watch that your dog does not get too tired: have "warming up" and "cooling down" periods such as 10-minute slow walks at each end of the exercise session.
■ On hot days carry water with you and exercise when it is cooler, in the early morning or evening.

> **"Regular exercise can help your dog to build strength and reinforce learning."**

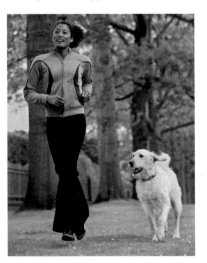

▲ **Exercise partners**
Going for a jog or run with your dog is great exercise for you both and can slot in with your usual daily routine.

▶ **Family fun**
Exercising your dog with the whole family can be a great deal of fun and will help build a strong bond with your pet.

■ In cold weather consider using a dog jacket for short-haired or elderly dogs to help keep their muscles warmer.

■ Don't let your dog run on hard surfaces if he is not used to it as he could hurt the pads of his paws. Similarly, avoid these surfaces if they are very hot or cold.

■ Take your dog's favourite toy or ball out on walks with you to encourage fun and energetic games of chase. These fun games are also good mental exercise for your dog.

■ Try to keep sessions at around the same time each day so that your dog learns to rest in between.

Walking and jogging

This type of exercise can be done almost anywhere. Jogging with your dog will help you both to keep fit. For his own safety and that of others, your dog needs to be able to walk calmly on a lead (pp.62–3).

Remember to carry bags with you to collect and dispose of faeces.

Free running

Running in open spaces is especially good exercise for high-energy or racing dogs such as Whippets and Greyhounds. First, in order to trust your dog to run a long distance from you, he needs to be trained to come reliably when you call him (pp.64–5). Find a large space such as a field, or beach without crowds. Check that there is no livestock that he could disturb. Make sure you are allowed to let your dog run freely in that area – many urban parks don't allow dogs off leads in certain places.

To ensure that your dog keeps you in mind while he is running around, play a few games of "hide and seek" or "fetch" with him (p.66). Agility games such as jumping over and running through obstacles can also be great exercise for your dog (pp.76–6).

Age and exercise

Your dog's need for exercise will change through his life.
■ Young pups can start going out once they are inoculated. Keep exercise sessions short.
■ For adult dogs, long walks and runs and energetic games are ideal. Pregnant bitches, or sick or convalescent dogs need only short, gentle exercise sessions.
■ Older dogs appreciate shorter, gentle walks, but may still enjoy learning new games.

Play time

Dogs are intelligent animals and play is very important for stimulating their minds. Playing with your dog can build your relationship, reinforce his training, and also help him learn how to get on with other dogs.

Types of games

Games can allow your dog or puppy to express his natural instincts in a fun way. Puppies who learn to play with other dogs are less likely to be timid or aggressive. Dogs particularly enjoy playing fetch, tug-of-war, and squeaky-toy games.

Fetch Chasing a ball or Frisbee is an excellent way for your dog to burn off energy. By bringing the toy back to you, the dog learns that he will get another go at chasing – and in the process he learns retrieval skills (p.66). Use toys rather than throwing sticks – your dog could

injure his mouth by catching a stick in the air or grabbing at a stick embedded in the ground.

Tug-of-war This game can be fun for both dogs and people, but bear in mind that "challenging" a person can sometimes become a bit too exciting for your dog. Use special "tug" toys (p.20). Make sure you win more often than the dog does. If he takes hold of your clothes or skin, stop playing immediately and quietly turn away from him.

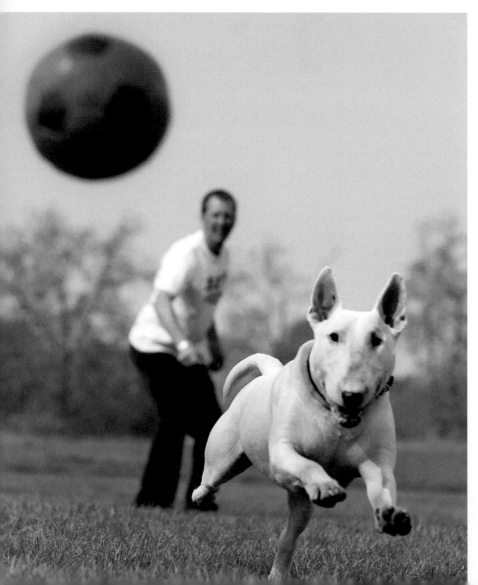

◄ **Fun exercise**
For games of fetch, take toys with you when you go for walks rather than using sticks. Playing "fetch" also encourages your dog to come to you when called.

Tips for play sessions

The following tips will enable you and your dog to get the most out of your play sessions:
- Keep play sessions short and varied so your dog will not get tired or overexcited.
- Make sure you decide when the play session starts and ends – this subtly reinforces your position as "pack leader".
- Remember that all toys are yours – dogs should always give up their toys when asked.
- Never encourage your dog to chase people. Humans should be friends and leaders, never "prey".
- Prevent play biting while your puppy is small – teach him to play with toys instead.
- Never let your dog jump up at people or grab things from them.

◄ **Tugging away**
Tug games are a favourite with many dogs –
especially terriers and competitive dogs. Dogs
enjoy the energy release and feelings of
strength that the game evokes.

■ Toddlers can be unnerving for dogs
as they may cry loudly and move
quickly and erratically. Gently
prevent your toddler from grabbing
at the dog, and make sure the dog
can escape.

■ Explain to children that puppies tire
easily and must be allowed to sleep if
they want to.

■ Dogs do not like to be disturbed
while they are eating. Don't let your
children play with or near a dog's
food or water bowl. Only an adult
should feed a dog.

■ As well as play, involve older
children in training your dog. With
the right support, children make
skilled and enthusiastic trainers.

Hide and seek This game satisfies a
dog's food-seeking instincts. Hide a
bit of food inside a toy, so your dog
has to scrabble and sniff around to
find it, or take several plastic cups
and hide some food under one of
them. You could also play hide and
seek with two people: one person
takes the dog's "fetch" toy (such as a
ball) and hides with it, while the other
holds the dog. The "hider" calls the
dog, and the other person lets the dog
go. When the dog finds the hider, this
person throws the toy for him. This
game is also a fun way to teach your
dog to come when called.

Squeaky toys Dogs bred to catch
small prey, and those with a strong
predatory instinct such as terriers,
enjoy playing with squeaky toys. The
squeak signifies the cry of an injured
animal and is especially appealing to

chase and catch. Some dogs may even
bite the toy to pieces until it stops
squeaking so make sure the toys don't
have small or sharp bits that could
cause choking.

Children and play

Dogs and children share a sense of fun
and love of life and they can become
the best of friends but they need time
to get habituated to one another.
Children can be a bit too rough with
dogs while playing, so all play and
interaction between them should be
supervised. Avoid a situation where
your dog is forced to retaliate and be
ready to step in to help when required.
The following guidelines should help
ensure everyone has fun safely:

■ Explain to your children that
playtime can be fun but they must not
tease a dog because this will upset him
and he may bite.

▲ **Playing together**
Children are full of enthusiasm and fun and can
make very good trainers. Well-socialized dogs
respond to them with excitement and energy
and enjoy their play sessions.

**"Games can allow your dog or puppy to
express his natural instincts in a fun way."**

Regular grooming

No matter what type of dog you have, regular grooming is essential to its health and wellbeing. Even short-coated dogs benefit from regular brushing, and choosing the right equipment will make grooming easier.

Grooming essentials

All dogs benefit from regular grooming, so make sure you leave time for it. As well as removing dead hair, grooming is good for the skin, and reduces the likelihood of your dog getting parasites such as fleas and ticks. The process is also a good opportunity to check your dog for any new lumps, bumps, or injuries that might need veterinary attention (pp.84–5). Grooming is relaxing for dogs, and helps to strengthen the bond between dog and owner.

Longer-coated dogs naturally require a lot of grooming – some breeds even need daily brushing.

▲ Grooming your dog
Whatever breed of dog you own, you should make sure you groom him regularly to avoid matted hair and to check for parasites.

Other short-haired breeds can be groomed as little as once a week. Whatever the length and texture of your dog's coat, it is advisable to groom him regularly. Knots and tangles that form in long coat are painful and difficult to remove once they have set in. Similarly, a build-up of dirt should be avoided, because it can quickly cause skin irritation.

When grooming a dog, special attention needs to be paid to the groin, ears, legs, and chest, where body parts rub across one another. These areas are prone to knots and tangles, particularly in breeds with long hair, such as Spaniels. You will

Coat types

There are a variety of different coat types, and each requires a different level of attention to maintain. Dogs with short, smooth, and wiry hair generally need less grooming than those with long, curly, or corded coats.

Short coat

Smooth coat

Wiry coat

Curly coat

Long-haired coat

Long silky coat

Corded coat

► **Grooming kit**
Your grooming kit will need to
contain some of the items
shown here. There are a range
of different tools available,
but some suit certain coat
types better than others.
Speak to a professional
groomer or breeder before
investing, to ensure you select
the right tools for your dog.
Clean your equipment after
each use to reduce the risk of
contamination.

Slicker brush

**Shedding
blade**

Comb

**Nail
clippers**

Rubber brush

Scissors

De-matting comb

Clippers

also need to focus closely on the
underside of your dog's feet and tail,
where dirt can easily build up.

While grooming is essential, it is
important not to get too carried
away. Be careful when using any tool
with metal teeth — being heavy-
handed or staying in one place too
long can cause cuts called brush
burns. Brushing is finished when all
the loose hair has been removed –
typically when it becomes difficult

to remove more than half a brush-
full of hair. Always approach
grooming in a calm, relaxed fashion
and without any force.

If your dog is uncomfortable for
any reason, for example when you
are removing a knot, take your time
and use treats to help him through

the experience. Using force may get
the job done quickly, but future
grooming sessions will become
much more difficult because your
dog will find them uncomfortable
and try to avoid them.

Tools of the trade

There are many grooming tools
available, and each boasts features to
make grooming more effective. It is
important to select a brush
appropriate for your dog's coat type.
For example, combs are available in a
variety of lengths, with and without
handles. Brush heads also come in a
range of shapes and sizes. Take some
time to select equipment that
you are comfortable handling and that
is appropriate for the size of your dog.

43

Regular grooming

> "Longer-coated
> dogs naturally
> require more
> attention than
> short-coated dogs,
> and some breeds
> need daily
> grooming."

Show coats

Owners who show their dogs take
grooming very seriously in order
to win. Several dog breeds are
expected to have amazingly
elaborate coat styles for the show
ring. These often require a great
deal of work by the owners to keep
the coat looking perfect. The
Yorkshire Terrier (seen right, at
show) and the Afghan Hound look
beautiful, but their coats can get
tangled very quickly and they
require constant attention to
maintain their appearance. Away

from shows, most pet owners
prefer to be more practical, and
clip their dog's coats into shorter
and more functional designs.

Washing your dog

An occasional bath can be great fun for your dog, especially if you get him used to it from an early age. Bathing is essential for a dog's skin and coat and keeps dirt, smells, and hair shedding to a minimum.

How often you should bathe your dog depends on what type of coat he has. Some long-haired dogs have a "double-coat" with a warm undercoat and thick guard hairs on the top. The guard hairs make double-coated dogs naturally dirt repellent, so they don't need to be bathed very frequently – twice a year is enough. Single-coated, short-haired dogs should be bathed more frequently – about once every three months. Curly coated dog breeds like Poodles do not shed their hair, and may need to be bathed more regularly, even as often as once a month. It is important not to wash any dog too often, as over-bathing causes the coat to compensate by producing extra oils, which in turn causes an increase of natural odour. If your dog gets muddy after a walk, he does not necessarily need a bath – just wait until the mud dries and then brush it off.

1
▲ Prepare for bath time
Lift your dog into the bath, then spend some time feeding him treats to make sure he is happy before you get him wet. Make sure you have dog shampoo, a towel, and a brush within easy reach so that you don't have to leave your dog unattended.

2
► Wet the coat
Test the water temperature before you start to wet your dog – it should be warm, but not hot. Beginning at the head, wet your dog fully from head to tail, being careful not to get water into his eyes, ears, and nose.

3

► Shampoo and massage

Apply dog shampoo and then massage it thoroughly into your dog's coat, right down to his skin.

4

◄ Rinse the shampoo out

Use warm water to thoroughly rinse all the shampoo out of your dog's coat. Any shampoo residue left in the coat will cause skin irritation.

5

▲ Dry the coat

Squeeze the excess water out of your dog's coat with your hands, then towel him all over, so that he is nearly dry. Finish by drying him fully with a hairdryer on low heat – as long as your dog isn't worried by the noise – brushing as you go.

Long-coated dogs

Dogs with long coats require more grooming than dogs with short coats. Essential tools for keeping their coats in good condition include a slicker brush, rake, comb and de-matting comb, and scissors.

Long-coated dogs should be groomed daily to stop tangles forming. Some breeds, such as Afghan Hounds, have extremely thin, silky hair, which tangles easily and forms knots. Others have hair that cannot fall out due to the length of the coat, causing it to form thick mats. Regular grooming will allow you to avoid these problems – you cannot rely on occasional trips to a professional groomer if you have a long-coated dog. Not only will your dog start to smell and look messy between visits, but removing the matted hair that builds up can be very painful for him. You will find it easiest to groom your dog when he is tired after a walk.

1
◄ De-matting comb
Mats can be difficult to remove and may cause pain to your dog because you will inevitably pull some hair out while removing them. To make de-matting easier, begin by breaking the mats into smaller manageable sections with a de-matting comb.

2
▲ Slicker brush
Once all of the big mats and knots have been removed, use a slicker brush to go over your dog's coat until there are no tangles left. Pay particular attention to the feathering around his legs.

4

▲ **Comb around the face**
Leave your dog's face until last, then spend some time carefully combing through the hair around the muzzle. A well-groomed dog will leave very little dead hair in a comb, which should pass through the coat easily.

3

▲ **Rake the coat**
Pick an area of coat, hold the rake lightly in one hand, and brush smoothly through the coat. Work systematically from head to tail along one side of your dog and then back up the other side.

"Long-coated dogs should be groomed daily to stop tangles forming."

Trimming around the feet (for long- and short-hair)

Hold the scissors flat against your dog's pad, then trim the coat so it is level with the base of the foot.

Then turn the foot over to trim around its top edges. Comb and trim the hair between the toes.

Short-coated dogs

Although they require less attention than long-coated breeds, short-coated dogs still benefit from regular grooming. A shedding blade and hairdryer are both effective for removing dead hair from a short-coated dog.

Short-coated dogs can be kept in perfect condition with just a two-minute daily brush and a thorough groom once a week. For your weekly session, start by using a hairdryer on a low heat to remove the dead hair from your dog's coat. Work in a systematic fashion to make sure no part of the coat is overlooked. Then use a shedding blade to pick up any remaining hair. Brushing should stop when all loose hair is removed from the coat – that is, when it becomes difficult to remove more than half a brush-full of hair. If you like, a damp towel or coat conditioner can then be used to add shine to the coat.

1
▲ **Bathing**
Short-coated dogs only need an occasional bath – about once every three months. They can be easily bathed at home; use a non-slip mat to keep your dog secure.

2
▲ **Using a hairdryer**
Hairdryers are an effective way of removing dead hair and dirt from short-coated breeds, though some dogs do not like the noise. If you use a hairdryer, it should always be on a low heat.

3

► **Shedding blade**
A shedding blade will pick up any remaining dead hair from your dog. Pass the blade lightly over the whole of his body, pressing gently and working with the direction of the coat.

▼ The finished article
Regular grooming means you and
your dog will both benefit from a
clean, odour-free coat that sheds
very little hair.

Wiry- and curly-coated dogs

Many owners of dogs with wiry and curly coats choose to take their pet to a professional grooming parlour. Alternatively, you can learn the necessary skills to groom your dog at home.

Hand stripping

Hand stripping is a method where the dog's hair is plucked from the root by hand. It is used for certain types of wiry haired breeds – typically working dogs such as Border Terriers and also for some show dogs. It is a very time-consuming method that is not always necessary for pet dogs. Hand stripping is best done when the dog's coat is naturally shedding, or "blown". This normally happens twice a year, and makes the process much easier and less stressful for the dog. Many experts prefer to use their fingers to pluck a few hairs at a time from across the whole coat. However, there are several tools available to make the process easier on both groomer and dog, such as a pumice stone, hand-stripping knife, shredder, and scissors.

1

▲ **Pumice stone**
The coarse texture of a pumice stone makes it perfect for removing the rough hair from a dog's top coat. The stone should be gently dragged over the top of the coat in the same direction as the hair.

2

▶ **Hand-stripping knife**
This is an excellent tool which can be used to remove the harsh topcoat from wiry coated breeds but is also used to "card" the undercoat – stripping out the shedding hairs quickly and easily.

3
▼ Shredder
There are many types of shredders available, some with large flexible blades and others with fixed teeth. In essence this is a serrated blade for removing the loose undercoat hair, while leaving the top coat intact.

4
► Scissors
Once all of the shedding hair has been removed, a dog can appear quite ragged. It is best to finish grooming by trimming his extremities to level out the coat. Then use thinning scissors to trim the finer hair around his legs and face.

Clipping

Clippers are an essential tool for grooming non-shedding, curly-coated breeds such as poodles. Many types of clippers are available, but the more money you spend the higher quality you can expect. Clippers take training and practice to use correctly. They should be held lightly between thumb and fingers, like a pencil. The amount of pressure you use and the position of the clippers should remain constant, otherwise the coat will be different lengths. Clipping should be done after a bath when the coat is clean and dry, because a very dirty or oily coat is impossible to clip.

► Using clippers
Choose a clipper blade appropriate for your dog. A "number 5" blade is a good overall choice and leaves the hair about 1cm (½in) long. Using guard combs may be a safer choice for an inexperienced groomer as there is less room for error.

Other grooming needs

It is not just your dog's coat that needs attention – his teeth, ears, and nails also need to be attended to regularly in order to keep your dog healthy and in the best possible condition.

Teeth cleaning

Dog's teeth benefit from weekly brushing, though you should only use dog-specific products. First, get your dog used to the feeling of having your hand resting across the bridge of his nose, with your thumb held under his chin to keep his mouth closed. Once he is comfortable with this, use your other hand to gently lift his top lip to reveal his teeth. If your dog remains calm, a toothbrush or fingerbrush can be inserted inside the cheek.

Teeth cleaning will be a strange experience for your dog at first, so use treats at each stage to put him at ease and encourage good practice in future. If he shows signs of aggression or anxiety during the process, stroke him slowly and gently for several minutes before trying again.

◄▲ Teeth brushing
The most important place to brush is along the gum line, as well as on the outside surfaces of all the teeth. Move the brush gently in a circular motion rather than scrubbing from side-to-side. You might find it easier to use a fingerbrush – a hollow plastic tube that fits over your finger and has in-built bristles. This can be a lot easier to manoeuvre around your dog's mouth and prevents you from applying too much pressure.

> "Teeth cleaning may be a strange experience for your dog so put him at ease."

Ear cleaning

Inspect your dog's ears regularly for any signs of discharge, unpleasant odour, redness, inflammation, or ear mites. Any of these symptoms may signal an infection, for which you should seek veterinary help (pp.100–1). Monthly ear cleaning will maintain the health of the ears and prevent infections. This is particularly important with drop-eared dogs such as Spaniels.

◄ Applying antiseptic ear cleaner
Antiseptic ear cleaner can be applied to cotton wool and used to wipe the visible areas of your dog's ears. Do not insert the cotton wool or any other object into your dog's ear canal.

Nail trimming

How often you will need to trim your dog's nails depends on his lifestyle and the dog itself, but monthly trimming should be enough for most. Nails need to be trimmed back as far as the "quick", which is where the blood vessels and nerves are. If you cut the nails too short, you will sever the quick, which will cause the nail to bleed extensively. Hold your dog's foot firmly to avoid him moving at the moment of cutting. Place the nail clippers just below the quick and cut the nail swiftly in one smooth movement. If you do cut the quick, remain calm and apply a small amount of styptic powder to the nail, applying firm pressure until the bleeding stops.

◄ Black nails
Dogs with black nails present a challenge as the quick can only be seen as a small white dot in the centre of the nail once you begin to trim. Trim only small sections at a time to prevent cutting through the quick.

▲ White nails
The quick is much easier to see on dogs with white nails than on dogs with black nails. It is a two-tone pink area in the centre of the nail, so make sure you clip below this point.

3

Training and behaviour

Being in charge

Having a well-behaved dog depends on building a good relationship with him. Learning to communicate the rules in a clear and calm way that your dog understands will ensure he responds positively to your requests.

Setting rules

Dogs are not naturally naughty – in fact they are deeply social animals who crave rules and boundaries. However, puppies are not born knowing what the rules are and even if you are starting to train an older dog, he may not yet have learnt all the rules you would like him to follow. Decide upon a set of rules you feel are important, then enforce them consistently through training methods such as reward-based training (p.59). Act quickly to stop any behaviour that breaks your rules; your dog will soon learn which behaviours are acceptable and which are not.

There is no need to prove your physical strength or dominance to enforce these rules. A good owner is calm, fair, and likeable – it is important to help your dog understand when he makes mistakes, without getting angry and shouting at him. Building a relationship with your dog based on mutual respect will make both owner and dog happier.

Your dog will gladly follow commands given by you as long as he understands what he needs to do. When training problems occur, it is usually because of poor communication. Since dogs have different motivations and needs than humans, taking time to understand how your dog learns and what signals he can follow will help set realistic expectations.

▲ **Happy together**
A healthy relationship is one where your dog is at ease because he knows what is expected of him as a pet, and where you enjoy the company of a dog who does as he is asked.

◄ **Clear communication**
Being a good dog owner is about learning how your dog interacts with the world and training him in ways that he is able to understand.

▲ ► Treats or toys as rewards
Treats should be small, soft, and smelly. They work best when they can be given quickly during training sessions and do not take your dog several minutes to eat. Favourite toys also make a great reward for playful dogs.

do not attempt this until your puppy has had plenty of practice already.

Reward-based training

Training your dog involves creating a situation where he is rewarded for certain behaviours instead of others. Any behaviour that is consistently rewarded will be repeated more often. This also means that bad behaviour, which is not rewarded, will soon disappear and be replaced by one that is rewarded. For your dog to understand how you want him to behave, give or withhold a reward at just the right time. Rewards can include food treats, games with toys, simple praise and affection, or even playing with other dogs. Remember that not all dogs find the same rewards appealing. Spend some time discovering what really

motivates your dog and use that as a reward. Giving a reward immediately following the behaviour you want means you will never need to use punishment methods while training.

One of the easiest reward-based ways of training is to use a food treat to lure your dog into the position you want him to be in. More complicated behaviours can be broken down and rewarded in stages, in a method called "shaping". So if you want your dog to sit, every time he moves closer to the ground and you reward him, he will realize what he is being asked to do. Getting rewarded for each small effort will make him repeat it. Maximize your training success by limiting his choices and thus preventing him from making the wrong decision. For example, train on a lead away from other dogs or in a room with no distractions.

Carry your dog's rewards with you whenever you plan to do some training. There is also a lot of

equipment you can buy to help you during training such as collars, leads, and harnesses. Choose equipment that is comfortable for both you and your dog to use and ask a professional to help you fit and use it correctly. However, always remember that while good equipment is necessary during training to keep your dog safe, avoid relying on tools too heavily. The day that you forget the equipment or it breaks, it will be the good training you have done that will prove most important.

Sit and stay

The most basic of training but also the most useful – the sit and stay commands – can help you control your dog in any situation. Most training and behaviour problems can be improved by teaching a reliable sit on command.

Sit

Dogs naturally sit of their own accord and it can be quite easy to simply reward them as and when it happens. However, taking the time to teach your dog to sit on command ensures he sits quickly and reliably in the face of any distraction. It is one of the easiest commands to teach and one that any dog will readily learn.

1
◀ **Dog in a stand**
Hold a treat in front of your dog's nose when he is standing in front of you. Lure him by moving the treat over his head so that he raises his nose.

3
▼ **Introduce hand signal**
Once your dog learns to sit, teach him to respond to a clear hand signal – an upward motion with a flat hand with palm facing up. After several repetitions, say "sit" a moment before the hand signal.

2
▲ **Feed treat and praise**
When your dog folds into the sit, release the treat and praise gently. Continue to praise and feed him treats if he remains sitting for longer.

> "Sit is one of the easiest commands to teach, and one any dog will readily learn."

Stay

Once your dog has learnt to sit on command, teach him to "stay", with your hand flat and palm facing down. You will feel more confident in an emergency situation if your dog obeys "sit" and "stay". These commands also help control unwanted behaviours. Unlike most basic training, teaching your dog to stay for long periods is best practised when he is tired, as he will be happy to rest in one position and more likely to remain still.

2

◄ Insert movement
When your dog has learnt to stay reliably, slowly move away from him by taking a step back and leaning your weight onto your back leg.

3

▼ Add distance
Move around your dog while he is sitting. If he moves to you, calmly reposition him and repeat. Gradually build up the distance away from him.

1

◄ Ask for sit
Ask your dog to sit, then hold your palm down and say "stay". Praise him immediately.

GOOD PRACTICE

After your dog has mastered the sit and stay, gradually teach him "down". From a sitting position, first lure him by bringing the hand with the treat in it all the way to the floor so that your dog follows it. As soon as his elbows are both on the ground, reward him immediately. Once he is reliably going straight down, introduce a clear hand signal – a downward motion with palm facing down – and again lure him into the down position. The next step is to train him to respond to your voice. Say "down" and then give your hand signal.

► Make him feel safe
Only ask your dog to lie down in environments where he feels safe, as dogs tend to feel vulnerable in the down position.

Walking on a lead

All dogs need to be walked on a lead at least some of the time to ensure their safety. Teaching your dog to do this without pulling will make going for a walk a more pleasant experience for you both.

Teaching a puppy to walk on a lead without pulling is easier than teaching an adult dog, who may have learnt all sorts of bad habits. However, no matter when you start the training, it is crucial to set rigid ground rules. As soon as your dog pulls you must stop walking and help him into the correct position by your leg. This can be very frustrating to begin with as you will be stopping every few paces. But by following the steps outlined here you can teach your dog where you want him to walk and reward him when he gets it right.

1

◄ Position the dog
Lure your dog into position using a treat in your left hand. Keep the treat low enough so he doesn't jump up, and the lead short enough that he can't wander off.

2

▼ Step forward
Keep your dog's attention by saying his name cheerfully and hold him in position against your leg, sitting or standing, with the treat.

3

▼ Treat in position

Take a step forward, stop and let your dog have the treat while he is in the correct position. If he stays by your side, take another step forward and reward him again.

4

►Practise

With each session, gradually increase the number of steps you take before rewarding your dog. If he moves away from you or gets distracted, lure him back into the correct position.

GOOD PRACTICE

Each new environment is likely to prove challenging for your dog so start each training session by rewarding one step at a time. As he gets good and is walking nicely for a few paces, progress to working with distractions in the distance such as other dogs. If he starts pulling or loses attention entirely, he probably isn't ready for this stage yet. Move the training to a quieter area and go back one stage.

Never get cross with your dog if he makes mistakes. Teaching him to walk without pulling takes time and you should plan longer walks to allow for the many stops you will have to make. Some dogs, especially older rescue dogs, are really dedicated "pullers" and basic training may be unsuccessful. In such cases it is best to seek the help of a professional dog trainer.

Resist the urge to use collars that tighten around your dog's neck. They do not teach your dog anything and have the potential to cause him serious damage.

► Come close

When training in a new environment for the first time, use special treats that your dog finds particularly tempting.

Come when called

The most joyful times you can have with your dog are outside, watching his enjoyment as he really stretches his legs. However, until your dog will reliably come when called, it is not safe to let him off the lead.

Training your dog to come when called should not be started on walks because there are simply too many temptations that may cause your dog to ignore you. However, by practising the following simple steps at home or in your garden, your dog will learn that coming back to you is always the better choice.

1

▶ **Show the treat to tempt him**
Get your dog focused on you by tempting him with his favourite treat. Let him sniff the treat but have a friend gently hold his collar so he can't reach to eat it.

2

▲ **Call him**
Keep your dog's attention on you and take a few paces away from him, then crouch down to your dog's level, throw your arms wide open, and call him with an enthusiastic "come". As you do this, your friend can let go of your dog's collar.

GOOD PRACTICE

Do not be tempted to call your dog over great distances to begin with as he may get distracted; he needs to be close enough to stay fixated on the treat.

However, if he doesn't come back to you immediately do not enter into a game of chase with him. Simply walk away and try training again later. No matter how long it has taken your

dog to come back to you, never tell him off when he does come back. He will not understand that you are angry because he has taken so long, he will only learn that coming back to you is a bad idea!

Once your dog has learnt to come every time you call him, you can gradually stop giving him his favourite treats and just use praise instead.

▲ **"Come to me"**
Your dog will learn to respond to your body language, so always keep your arms wide and welcoming when calling.

3

▼ Encourage him with a treat

As soon as your dog is within a couple of feet of you, hold out the treat as a lure and tempt him to come right up to you. Tease him a bit with the treat – you don't want him to grab the treat and run off.

"Good boy!"

4

► Reward and praise

As you feed him the treat, gently take hold of his collar with your other hand and tickle his chin. Praise him and feed him some more treats so he learns that coming back to you is really beneficial.

Fun training

Training does not need to stop at obedience commands such as sit. Some of the most fun training you can do with your dog involves teaching games such as fetching toys, or learning amusing tricks.

Fetch

One of the most enjoyable games for a dog to learn is how to fetch a toy on command. It also helps him get good exercise without you having to move. No dog is born knowing how to retrieve so it's necessary to teach him the rules of the game first.

1

▲ **Build excitement**
Start by holding your dog's favourite toy. Make lots of enthusiastic noises and tease him by moving the toy around.

2

▶ **Throw the toy**
When he is well and truly interested in the toy, throw it a short distance in front of him so that he races to get it.

3

◀ **"Good dog!"**
Praise your dog as soon as he picks the toy up but do not try to take it from him. This will only make him want to run away to play with his prize on his own. Give him even more praise, and even a food treat, if he returns the toy to you.

Wave

Teaching tricks is a great way to bond with your dog and keep him interested in training. Giving a paw, which is easily turned into a wave, is a great trick and will impress any visitors. Keep sessions short and always go back a step if your dog jumps up, and praise and reward even the slightest attempt to wave. Once he has mastered waving, develop it into the hi-five (see panel, below).

1
▲ Giving a paw
Hold a treat and make a fist so that your dog can smell the treat but cannot reach it. Put your fist on the floor and encourage him to investigate. Praise any attempt to use his paw.

2
▲ Move fist up
When your dog understands he has to touch your hand with his paw to release the treat, slowly move your fist away from the floor.

3
► Wave
Over successive training sessions move your fist higher and higher so your dog has to reach his paw up and "wave" to earn the treat.

GOOD PRACTICE

When your dog is performing these tricks confidently, introduce a voice cue by giving a command a moment before giving your hand signal. Continue to use treats until he is reliably responding to your voice cue alone. Teach him to distinguish between the voice cues of the wave and the hi-five (see right).

Once your dog can wave or hi-five confidently with you kneeling in front of him, try teaching him to respond to your commands while you stand. Reward your dog well each time he gets it right.

► Hi-five
Turn the wave into a hi-five by stretching out your hand. As your dog lowers his paw, let it land against your palm. Support the paw lightly rather than holding it as he may find this threatening.

Training classes

Training classes are an excellent way to teach your dog good behaviour. They are also a good way to meet other like-minded people and learn about the facilities your local area has to offer dog owners.

When to consider classes

No matter what your experience of training dogs, classes are advisable for any new dog – whether it be a puppy or an older, rescued dog. The benefits dogs receive from taking part in a group class are enormous and it is also a good way to hone your skills. All dogs are different and will benefit from slightly varied approaches in their training. Furthermore, having an experienced trainer on hand will prevent you from making mistakes. It is also much easier to keep motivated when training as part of a group.

However, nervous dogs and those who are aggressive towards people or other dogs are not suitable for group classes. These types of behavioural problems are often aggravated in a class situation and can become more pronounced. Quite often these dogs are better starting off in a one-to-one training session, with someone who is qualified in dealing with behavioural problems, before progressing into a group class. If you have any concerns, enquire before enrolling your dog.

Where to train

There are likely to be several classes running in your area. Try to get recommendations from other dog owners or your vet. Choose a trainer who is recognised by an official organisation such as the Association of Pet Dog Trainers. Before you choose a class, take the time to visit and watch a training session take place. Even if you have no experience of training classes, you will quickly get a feel for a good class. Aim for classes with relaxed dogs and happy owners. Avoid hectic and noisy environments.

What to look for

- Smaller classes with fewer dogs.
- High trainer-to-dog ratio.
- Positive training methods utilizing praise, food, and toys.
- No choke chains.
- No aggressive training.
- A relaxed environment.

"The benefits dogs receive from taking part in a group class are enormous and it's a good way to hone your skills."

◄ **Training classes**
Training classes should be well organized and enjoyable for all the owners and dogs present. A knowledgeable and experienced trainer will take charge in a friendly and effective manner.

Obedience heelwork
All training classes teach the basic skill of getting your dog to walk to heel. If you can keep your dog by your side in a controlled environment you will soon be able to walk him in public spaces with confidence.

Behavioural problems

Most dogs who are trained in basic rules from a young age happily integrate into their household. However, some dogs develop unwanted behaviours throughout their lives that require further training.

Destructive behaviour

Chewing is a natural behaviour in dogs, but when it becomes excessive or is targeted towards something inappropriate it can quickly become a source of tension between an owner and their dog. There are some common reasons why a dog may become destructive. For example, puppies will naturally chew on things out of curiosity and this behaviour becomes more pronounced while they are teething. However, this tendency disappears with age and consistent training. Sometimes dogs become destructive as an outlet because they are experiencing physical pain or because they are suffering from a genuine separation anxiety disorder. Much like humans, dogs can develop mental illnesses however supportive and happy their home life. Separation anxiety in dogs is a recognized condition characterized by extreme distress during the absence of their owner. It is imperative that advice about this condition is sought from your vet in combination with a professional behaviourist.

Occasionally destructive behaviour such as chewing or digging can become a problem in otherwise healthy, adult dogs. Quite often this is a sign that the dog is not being sufficiently stimulated or may not have an outlet for the behaviour elsewhere and is feeling frustrated. Terriers, for example, have been bred to dig and allowing them to exhibit

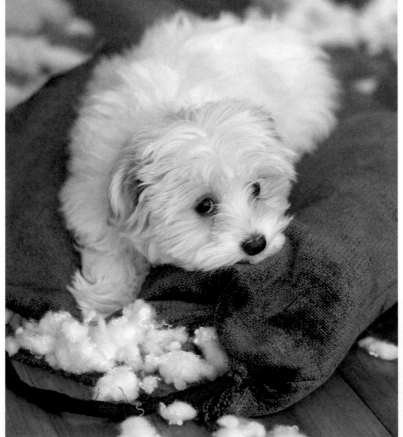

◄ Dealing with chewing
Puppies naturally use their mouths to investigate their environment but you should never punish them for this or they will learn to hide from you when they are chewing.

▼ Biting problems
Puppies "play bite" humans in the same way they do other puppies and this is best discouraged early on. If your puppy gets too excited, simply walk away.

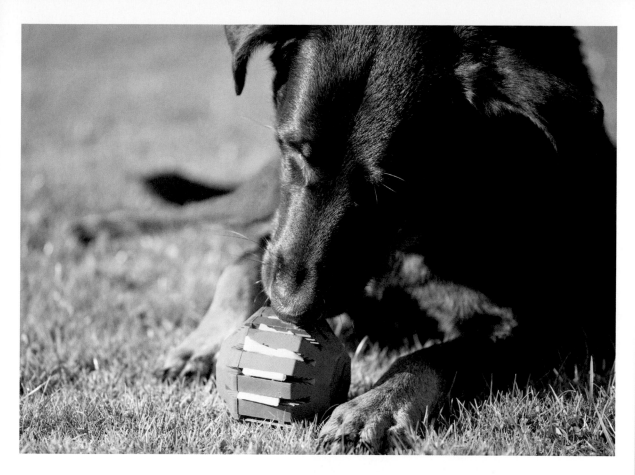

this behaviour by searching for treats in a particular area – such as a sand-pit – can save the rest of your garden. This will only work in dogs where all of their other needs such as physical exercise, nutritional requirements, and social interaction are met.

Problem solving

In order to tackle such destructive behaviours, first you must decide how you are going to allow your dog to perform the behaviour in an acceptable way. For example, a dog that chews furniture can be taught to chew special toys containing food instead.

The first stage of training is to put the desired behaviour on cue, by associating a command word with the behaviour. For example, offer your dog a toy with some treats hidden inside and praise him as he begins to investigate it, telling him "good boy, chew" in a clear voice. During this training it is vital that you make some temporary changes to restrict your dog's opportunities to perform the unwanted behaviour. If the behaviour you are trying to eliminate is chewing furniture, do not allow your dog to wander in the house unsupervised. If that is impractical, look into other preventatives such as a bitter spray to

▲ Chew toys
Chew toys, some of which can hold treats, can be used to tackle a huge range of problem behaviours. It is wise to get your puppy used to having quiet time with their toys every day.

make the furniture taste unpleasant.

When you have made a good association between the cue word and the correct behaviour, you have a channel of communication when your dog misbehaves. Resist the urge to punish your dog in this situation. He is not being naughty – he just needs to chew and cannot be expected to know the difference at first between your furniture and his toys. If you catch him chewing the furniture, simply interrupt him (for example with a hand clap) and hand him his chew toy, saying "good boy, chew".

"A dog that chews furniture can be taught to chew food toys instead."

Barking and jumping up

The most common behavioural problems associated with dogs are barking and jumping up at people. Both of these can be very cute in puppies but soon become irritating when they extend into adulthood.

Barking

Excessive barking is a behaviour that can quickly become a problem within a household and can cause tensions with neighbours, too. As is so often the case with commonly occurring behavioural problems, barking is a completely normal dog behaviour. They are genetically predisposed to do it and therefore it is unfair to expect a dog never to bark. However, it is perfectly reasonable to teach them to bark in moderation and only in certain circumstances. Bear in mind that dogs sometimes bark incessantly when shut in a room or in the garden for long periods. In this case, your dog's routine should be changed to allow them more freedom, which will result in reduced barking.

The easiest way to control problem barking is to train your dog to bark on command and follow this with teaching "be quiet" on command as well. Teaching a dog to "speak" is a great game and one that most dogs who already like to bark take to very quickly. Start by doing something that would normally cause your dog to bark, such as waving a toy or knocking at the door. When you have discovered a reliable way of encouraging your dog to bark, insert the command to "speak" just before they bark. Praise them for barking

◄ **Beware of the dog**
Dogs will often bark at people or other dogs passing their territory. Although their intentions may be friendly, this can appear intimidating to some people and should be discouraged.

▲ Anti-barking measures
If your dog persistently barks at passers-by or strangers on his territory, then try pulling curtains across windows to restrict his view.

► Don't pay attention
Do not give your puppy any fuss or attention if he jumps up. Only praise him when he has all four paws on the floor again.

and then approach them and hold a treat in front of their nose to stop them barking. Then simply say the word "quiet" and feed them the treat. Training sessions can be repeated several times throughout each play session, and are best ended with a fun game of tug or similar.

Never start this training, however, if your dog is barking out of aggression. If your dog barks sharply at people or other dogs this is an aggression issue (p.75), and a professional behaviourist will need to be involved.

> "Save time and effort by teaching young puppies not to jump up from the first day you take them home."

Jumping up

Jumping up is probably the most commonly complained-about behavioural issue and is the one problem that owners are most guilty of creating themselves. Puppies naturally tend to jump up to try to get closer to people's faces and hands, which they recognize as the sources of affection from humans. It is natural to encourage this because it seems cute and fun when puppies do it. However, before long they will have doubled in size and their habit of jumping up becomes annoying, painful, and potentially dangerous. It is possible to save a lot of time and effort later on in life by teaching young puppies not to jump up from the very first day you take them home.

However, if you have an older dog who already habitually jumps up at people you will need to train him that this is unacceptable. This can be as simple as following the instructions to

teach a "sit" (p.60). A dog that is sitting cannot jump up and therefore the problem is solved. In practice, if the urge to jump up is irresistible to your dog, it may be necessary to set up specific training sessions to solve the problem. To do this, put him on a short lead and get a friend to walk slowly towards you. When you have your dog sitting obediently, your friend can approach and give him praise but must move away again if he gets over-excited and jumps up.

As training progresses, you should be able to take off the lead but your dog will still need to be reminded to "sit". It is imperative that everyone enforces the rule not to let him jump up or your training will fail. Do not make the mistake of becoming complacent when praising your dog for sitting obediently. If he is not getting any praise for sitting politely, he is very likely to jump up as a way of getting lots of attention again.

Running away and aggression

Despite your best efforts, it's possible that your dog might develop a serious behavioural problem. The most common and potentially dangerous examples are a dog that runs away and a dog that responds to situations aggressively.

Running away

All dogs love being able to run free, really stretching their legs and playing with toys or other dogs. However, until your dog will return to your call then it is not safe to let him off his lead. You may come across someone who isn't confident around dogs or perhaps meet another dog who is not friendly. Often dogs learn to run away from their owners because they have been allowed to play off the lead before they have properly learned to come when called. Dogs habitually run away from their owners for a variety of reasons. Do not take it personally, simply remind yourself that your dog spends all day in a house with you and is finding the temptations of the outside world too distracting. In this case it is likely that your dog views returning to you as a signal that his fun is about to end and is therefore best avoided. If your dog finds running away more rewarding than staying with you, training must focus on ensuring your dog not only comes back to you but also enjoys spending play time with you.

If your dog will not return to you in a distraction-free environment such as your home or garden, it is too much to expect him to come back on a walk. Go back to basics and practise "come when called" at home in a quiet environment (pp.64–5). You can introduce recall training to many elements of your daily life; try recalling him to a food bowl at dinner time, or recall from a thrown toy. Remember to always give lots of praise when he comes back to you.

Once your dog will return to you quickly and happily in and around the house, it is time to move the training outside. Walk your dog on his normal lead, but have a light, long lead attached as well and tuck it away in your pocket. When you get to a safe, open space you can make a big show

▲ Runaway dog
The outside world can be full of temptations for your dog. You should always practise recall training with your dog in a quiet, controlled environment at home before you let him off the lead during walks.

▶ Returning for treats
Dogs should be taught that coming back when called means that they get a reward and are then allowed to continue playing. Only occasionally does it signal the end of the walk.

Aggression

Aggression is a natural canine response when a dog is not comfortable in a situation. However, for pet dogs to be trustworthy in all situations they must understand that aggression is not an acceptable response towards humans or other dogs. By the same logic, a good owner needs to take note of when a dog is becoming distressed and take steps to help him be more comfortable in that situation, thus reducing the risk of an aggressive response in the first place. However, most happy and well socialized dogs are not aggressive other than in rare cases where they are injured and in pain or surprised while sleeping.

Never challenge an aggressive dog. If a dog is growling at you, they are telling you that they are unhappy and want you to move away. Pinning them to the floor, shouting at them or any other harsh treatment will only result in the dog becoming more aggressive over time as they feel the need to defend themselves.

> ## "Aggression is a natural canine response but it is rare in happy, well socialized dogs."

of taking your dog's lead off. He will assume he is off the lead, but in actual fact you have hold of the end of the long-line. Do not use this as you would a lead – it is simply your safety line. You should aim to leave it dragging along the ground and avoid it pulling taut. Now try calling your dog as you have practised at home: say your dog's name, followed by "come", stand up tall and wave your arms with a big smile on your face! Your dog should want to come back to you, because he knows he will get treats or praise every time he does.

Keep the training varied – ask him to recall many times and be totally unpredictable with when you call him. Treat him sometimes, play with him others. Occasionally put him back on the lead for a little while and then let him off for a free run again. Keep him with you for a minute or two, then next time call him and send him straight off again. The key is to always praise the recall in some way.

Controlling risks

Aggressive dogs are not only a risk to yourself and other humans but also fellow dogs. Do not attempt to remedy the problem without professional help. First, ensure you put control measures in place, such as keeping your dog muzzled and on a lead when out, and then speak to your vet about getting a professional, accredited dog behaviourist to assist you.

Competitions and sports

Becoming involved in further training provides fun and satisfaction for both you and your dog while strengthening your bond. There are many sports you can take part in and competitions you can enter with your dog.

Dog shows

There are a number of different activities to choose from but before you start make sure to register with the appropriate governing body and familiarize yourself with the rules. Many people choose to first enter their dogs in a breed show. However it is easy to get put off if your dog does not do as well as you think he should. You can improve your chances of success by finding a good ringcraft training class run by experienced breeders and handlers from the show world. In many parts of the world there are also companion dog shows, which tend to be smaller and less daunting shows for beginners.

An alternative to breed showing are less competitive, pet-friendly obedience competitions. Dogs are required to perform a series of obedience tasks such as walking on a loose lead and going to their bed. These competitions are usually structured by levels of increasing difficulty and dogs are judged on their ability to complete tasks including heelwork, stays, retrieve, and recall. Dogs who earn a gold award are recognized as being very obedient.

When looking for a local obedience club to train with, be sure to find one that uses only positive training methods like those outlined in this book.

Agility

An increasingly popular alternative to standard obedience competitions is canine agility. Dogs learn to negotiate a range of obstacles and winning requires a high level of training skill as well as speed. Dogs never seem to tire of jumping over hurdles or through hoops, running through tunnels, weaving through poles, and balancing along the seesaw. Success depends on the amount of practice you are prepared to put in with your dog with many competitors owning their own agility equipment or attending a training club several times a week. Canine agility is not recommended for young puppies

▲ In tandem
Heelwork to music is enjoyed both by dog and owner. It requires them to be fit and supple and work in perfect harmony.

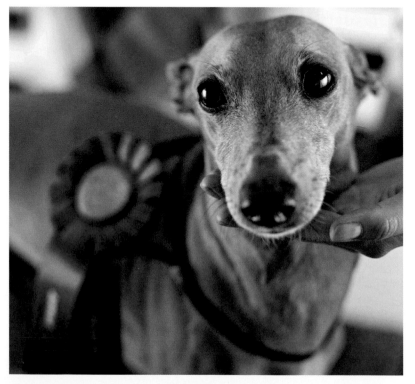

◄ Wonderful win
The pleasure of winning your first rosette with your dog is something you will remember for many years to come.

▲ Weave poles
Weave poles are one of the most difficult obstacles for dogs to master. It requires them to weave in and out at speed without missing any of the poles.

▲ Tunnels and jumps
Tunnels vary in height and style with some placed in such a way that the exit is not visible to the dog. Jumps also vary and require dogs to judge distance and height carefully.

as their growing bones and joints can be damaged by jumping. Dogs need to be at least 18 months of age to be allowed to compete.

Variations

As dog sports have become more popular in recent years, several variations on obedience and agility training have appeared. Rally obedience (Rally-O) with its informal feel and variety of freestyle exercises is emerging as a favourite sport. Unlike traditional obedience competitions, handlers follow a predetermined route as opposed to following the judge's orders and they are allowed to encourage their dogs. Yet another alternative is freestyle and heelwork to music – otherwise known as dancing with your dog. With practice the routines can look extremely impressive with jumps,

> "Dogs never seem to tire of jumping over hurdles or through hoops, running through tunnels, and weaving through poles."

twists and turns, and even walking on two legs. However, in essence these are obedience moves taught one at a time and put together to fit a music track. There are many beginner courses available at training clubs to get you started.

An increasingly popular alternative to agility is flyball, which involves teams of dogs racing each other and jumping over hurdles to press the flyball box. This action releases a ball, which the dogs must then return to the start. Flyball suits toy-orientated, social, and energetic dogs who enjoy retrieving. For those dogs not suited to working as part of a team, there are disc sports such as Frisbee-catching. Dogs earn marks for catching the Frisbee over increasing distances and even earn extra points for style.

Trials and events

Working and gun dog trials take a high degree of training but are a hugely rewarding way to release your dog's potential. Not all dogs are suitable so if you are interested it is worth speaking to an expert first.

Working trials

These trials are loosely based on the training police dogs undergo and appeal to many trainers due to the variety of exercises and less formal assessment involved. Dogs must progress through increasingly difficult challenges to move up to the highest level. All of the tasks are divided into control, agility, and nose work categories.

The control round includes heelwork, retrieve, speak on command, send-away, stays, and steadiness to gunshot. The agility stage involves jumping a hurdle and long jump as well as scaling a wall.

▲ Herding
Dogs that are bred to herd livestock will often develop behavioural problems if they are not given a suitable outlet for their herding instincts. Herding trials are perfect for these breeds.

▶ Sled dogs
Many dog breeds were created for the sole purpose of pulling sleds. Sled dogs such as Huskies get huge satisfaction from doing what they were bred for.

The nose work is split between a search square – where dogs must locate any object carrying human scent within a given area – and a tracking exercise. Tracking is where a dog follows the path walked by a person, possibly several hours before. The dog is required to use his nose to detect ground particles or any other disturbance left by the track-layer.

Gun dog trials

If you own a gun dog breed such as a Labrador Retriever your dog is likely to love bringing objects back to you. Gun dog trials or field trials (which are very similar but do not actually involve shooting game) test a dog's ability to fulfil the role of a working gun dog. Tests include flushing and retrieving game as well as the necessity for gun dogs to remain under control around guns at all times.

Other events

There are a variety of other niche sports suitable for particular breeds, such as water rescue events for Newfoundland dogs and their crosses; racing for Afghan Hounds; tracking tests for Bloodhounds; and carting for Bernese Mountain Dogs.

There are also many different endurance events for all breeds but only the most fit and active dogs can participate. These activities include dog hiking, cani-cross (cross-country running with your dogs), joring (biking or skiing with your dogs), sled-dog racing, and protection sports such as Schutzhund, where dogs are taught to search out and apprehend "criminals". All of these sports will improve your dog's physical and mental wellbeing. But more importantly, the enjoyment you will both receive from working together is immeasurable.

Gun dogs
Unlocking your dog's true potential will be a real thrill for both him and you. Gun dogs take naturally to the work, as they are bred specially for this reason. The real skill is inserting control and enthusiasm.

4

Your dog's health

Signs of good health

A healthy dog is easy to recognize by the way he looks and behaves, allowing for individual variation, breed, and age. Once you get to know your own dog, you should have no difficulty in judging if all is well.

Healthy appearance

Bright eyes, a glossy coat, and a cold wet nose may be cited as classic signs of good health in a dog, but these are not invariable rules. A dog's bright eyes may dim with age, even if he stays perfectly fit; his coat will not look glossy if it is wire-haired; and a healthy dog can have a warm dry nose.

Perhaps more useful fitness indicators are your dog's body shape and weight, which should stay consistent: strange swellings, sudden loss of weight, and abdominal bloating are all possible early health warnings. Monitor weight gain and growth in a young dog by weighing him weekly and plotting the weight on a graph; back up this data by taking regular photographs as he matures.

Changes in health are also revealed in a dog's faeces and toileting habits, which can be markedly different from one dog to another. As you clear up after your dog, it will become obvious what is normal for him in terms of frequency, consistency, and colour.

Healthy behaviour

- Looks bright and alert
- Interacts readily with family and other pets
- Moves freely, without stiffness
- Eager to take exercise
- Not unduly tired by exercise
- Interested in food
- Drinks expected amount of water
- Urinates and defecates to normal pattern

> "A cold wet nose may be cited as a classic sign of health but it is not an invariable rule."

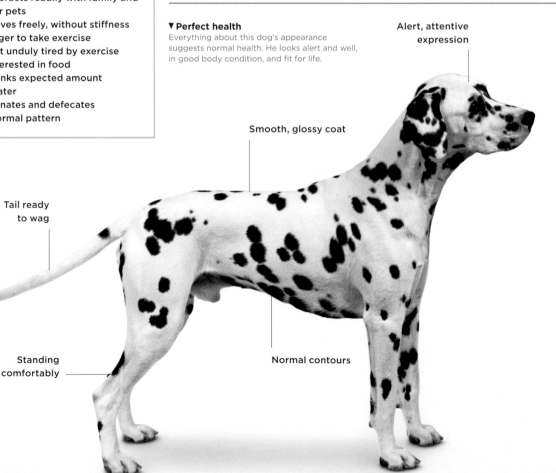

▼ **Perfect health**
Everything about this dog's appearance suggests normal health. He looks alert and well, in good body condition, and fit for life.

Alert, attentive expression

Smooth, glossy coat

Tail ready to wag

Normal contours

Standing comfortably

Home checks

From early puppyhood, accustom your dog to routine checks in which you examine each part of his body. Noticing the slightest change could allow early diagnosis of a health problem, and potentially a better outcome.

While examining each part of your dog's body, talk to him to boost his confidence and use commands such as "teeth" and "ears". Look first for any obvious changes in body shape and stance, then go over him in more detail, searching for cuts, lumps, and external parasites (pp.120–1). Run your hands over and under his head and body, down all four legs, and along the length of his tail. Part the fur in places, especially over his rump; hopefully, you will find no evidence of fleas or flea dirts, there should be little or no debris, and the coat should feel and smell pleasant. Stroking your dog should be a good experience for both of you.

Tips on handling

- ■ Make the experience positive
- ■ Give treats
- ■ Praise your dog
- ■ Handle each body part from ears to tail
- ■ End with lots of fuss

▲ Eyes
There should be no excessive tear production or sticky discharge. A little "sleep" is normal – simply wipe it away, using a separate piece of damp cotton wool for each eye. Gently lower the bottom eyelids to check that the lining and the white around the irises are not inflamed and red.

▶ Ears
Your dog should not find it painful to have his ears touched. There should be no swelling of the flaps, and the ears should be clean as far down as you can see and pleasant smelling.

▲ Teeth

Your dog should accept you looking in his mouth and brushing his teeth. Raise the upper lips to reveal the outer surfaces of the teeth. Ideally, these should be white but light brown tartar may accumulate. The gums should be moist and pale pink, and the breath smell pleasant.

▼ Paws

Train your dog from a young age to allow his paws to be lifted up and examined. Look between the toes for grass awns and bright orange harvest mites. Check for swellings and broken or overly long claws; when fully weight-bearing the claws should just touch the ground.

▲ Tail

Look under the tail at the anus for soiling and swellings, and in a bitch check the vulva for swelling and discharges. Examine the penis of a male dog for injuries and excessive discharge or bleeding from the tip.

Puppy health checks

If you have not owned a pet before, you need to register with a veterinary practice. Your choice could be based on the suggestions of friends, local advertising, or Internet searches for practices in your area.

First puppy check

Take your puppy for his first veterinary check as soon as is convenient. Unless he is already fully vaccinated, carry him into the practice, wearing a collar and lead in case he jumps out of your arms, and keep him off the floor. Alternatively, put him in a pet carrier. There are likely to be other owners with animals in the waiting room and it can be noisy, so give your puppy lots of reassurance.

Vets enjoy meeting puppies, and you are likely to receive a warm welcome.

The vet will ask you for details of your puppy's early life: his date of birth; the size of the litter; how your pup compared with his littermates; where and how the pups were reared; what worming and flea treatments were carried out; and the results of any screening tests for the breed. If your puppy has been vaccinated, show the vet the certificate.

The vet will scan your puppy to check he has been microchipped (see box, opposite), weigh him, and make a detailed examination, including

checking his ears with an auroscope and listening to his heart. If a vaccination is required, it will be given now. You may need to make some follow-up appointments to complete the vaccination course and to allow the vet to monitor your puppy's progress (see p.85).

Before you leave, the vet should offer advice on diet, worm and flea control, neutering, socializing and training, and travelling in the car. Do not hesitate to ask if you need any further information.

▼ **Meeting the vet**
Your puppy should be relaxed and enjoy his first appointment at the veterinary practice. Reassure him whilst the vet examines him, and take the opportunity to ask any questions you may have.

> "Vets enjoy meeting puppies, and you are likely to receive a warm welcome."

▲ Avoid confusion
If you give a voice command at the same time as a hand signal, your dog will tend to learn the hand signal but ignore the voice command.

▲ Staying focused
Don't get angry if your dog gets distracted by his environment. Instead do something to turn his attention back to you. Using treats or a toy, even a game of chase, will all help to re-engage him.

Voice and hand commands

Your voice is a useful training tool but it is easy to forget that dogs cannot understand spoken language. Your dog is capable of remembering what certain words sound like and what he should do when he hears them but only after repeated training and only if those words always sound the same. Asking your dog to "sit" one day and "sit down" the next will confuse him and make training more difficult. The tone of your voice is also very important. Your dog will use your tone to gauge whether he is doing the right thing or not, so always keep your voice cheerful when teaching new words.

Your dog will also look at your body posture to work out the context of a situation and what you are asking him to do. However, just as dogs have no concept of language, they do not understand that by pointing at something you are trying to direct their attention to somewhere other than the end of your hand.

Dogs and especially puppies find learning hand signals easier than learning voice commands, as only a small part of their brain can process verbal information. Once your puppy has learnt the hand signal and is responding reliably to it every time, add a voice command ahead of the hand signal. Eventually, after lots of repetitions, your dog will respond to the voice command alone.

Remember, your dog can only concentrate on one thing at a time. Be patient while training and ensure that your dog has fully learnt one command before trying to teach him a new one.

Pack behaviour

Dogs are pack animals and, like humans, they seek out social companionship and build strong relationships. Also because their ancestors once lived in packs, dogs look up to a leader they can respect and follow. Without a strong leader they can turn unruly. Giving approval through praise and affection will make your dog feel secure and loved. If he senses you are angry or distracted, he may become fearful or withdrawn.

Basic training

Training should be an enjoyable experience for both you and your dog. These pages will get you started but if you are unsure always seek the help of a professional dog trainer sooner rather than later.

When to train

There are many things to consider while training but the most important is to choose the right time. Aim to train for a few minutes several times a day as this will get much better results than a longer training session once a day. Choose times when you are not stressed or in a rush otherwise your dog will sense your tension and be far more likely to get things wrong in his attempts to please you.

Equally important is to consider your puppy's mood. Trying to train an over-excited puppy who hasn't had much exercise will be difficult. And a puppy who has just eaten a large meal will feel sleepy and will not be particularly motivated by food treats. Start training him in a quiet, distraction-free environment such as your living room, especially when attempting to teach new or difficult commands. You may want to build up to training in high-distraction environments such as a local park but

"Training your dog involves creating a situation where he is rewarded for certain behaviours instead of others."

◄ **Indoor training**
Begin training indoors away from distractions of the outside environment. When you do move training outside, start somewhere quiet and enclosed, far from other dogs and people.

▲ Checking limbs
The vet will examine each leg in turn, feeling along the bones and checking joint movement. This helps to detect hereditary conditions such as hip dysplasia at an early stage.

► Checking ears
Using an auroscope, the vet can make a deep examination of the ear. A common problem in puppies is infestation with ear mites, which can often be seen moving around; your vet will prescribe the appropriate treatment.

Follow-up puppy check

The veterinary practice may suggest that you take your puppy for a further check-up when he is four or five months old, to ensure that he is growing and developing well, both physically and socially. This will also give you the chance to build on the advice given at the first puppy appointment. At such a follow-up check, the vet will look for any puppy teeth that were not shed as the adult versions came through. This is important, as the baby teeth may need to be removed to allow the adult teeth to take up the right position within the mouth and ensure the correct bite.

Asking about neutering

If you plan to have your dog neutered, as the majority of owners decide to do, an early puppy health check is a good opportunity to ask for advice. Your vet will explain what the procedure involves for either a dog or a bitch and suggest when neutering is

◄ Flea combing
A severe infestation of fleas can be serious in a young puppy. Your vet will run a fine-toothed comb through the puppy's coat to catch any live fleas or pick up flea dirts.

Microchipping

Compulsory in England as of 6th April 2016, and later in the year throughout Britain, implanting a microchip under the skin between your puppy's shoulders – a procedure rather like giving a vaccination – ensures that he can always be identified. Scanning the chip reveals a unique number against which any contact information you have provided is recorded in a central database.

best carried out. Veterinary opinions differ as to the ideal time for dogs to be neutered, with the recommended age ranging from a few weeks to a few months. Most commonly, the operation is performed after puberty. Many owners worry about the after-effects of neutering and any concerns you may have can also be discussed with the vet at your puppy's health check.

Routine veterinary checks

Taking an adult dog for a regular health check is rather like taking a car for its annual service. This is when hidden problems are picked up and minor issues can be dealt with before they become major worries.

▲ Making sure all is well
The annual check can be quite a social time for you, your dog, and the vet. This is your chance to discuss any concerns you may have.

► Checking movement
The vet will move your dog's joints, identifying any pain, stiffness, and reduced range of movement which may be signs of arthritis.

Annual check

If you plan to take your dog for an annual check you will need to book an appointment in advance. The normal routine is for the vet to examine your dog from head to tail and ask various questions – for instance, about his thirst, appetite, diet, toileting habits, and exercise. If there is any cause for concern, detailed diagnostic tests may be recommended. You may be asked to take a sample of your dog's urine to the appointment, particularly if your pet is a senior, as this will provide additional important information about the kidneys and bladder. The sample should be collected early that morning into a suitable container (not a jam jar).

Your vet will also be able to advise on general health matters such as weight, body and coat condition, and control of worms, fleas, and other parasites. If your dog has a microchip it will be checked with a scanner.

"The normal routine is for the vet to examine your dog from head to tail and ask various questions. If there is any cause for concern, diagnostic tests may be recommended."

Vaccination stimulates immunity against serious infectious diseases, and usually requires regular boosters. The vaccine is given by a relatively painless injection under the skin.

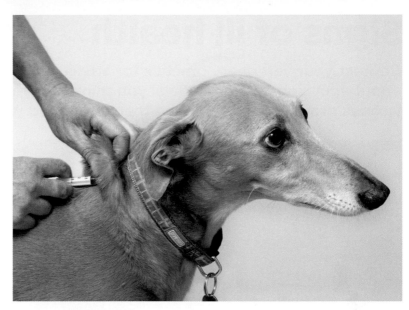

Other routine procedures may include clipping the claws if they are overgrown, and giving booster vaccinations to maintain protection against infectious diseases.

Some dogs do not like being examined, or resent a particular procedure, such as ear examination. If this is the case, the vet may suggest muzzling your dog, or ask you to go out of the room and have a vet nurse assist because some dogs are braver and better behaved away from their owners.

Some veterinary practices also run specific clinics, such as those dealing with dental or weight issues. These may be run by a veterinary nurse, who will refer you to a veterinary surgeon if a potential problem is detected.

Dental check

A healthy mouth not only enables your dog to enjoy eating his food but is also important for his general well-being, as decayed teeth and infected gums can lead to diseases in other parts of the body. The teeth will be examined as a matter of routine at annual checks and any

interim visits, but you may want to consider taking your dog to a regular dental clinic. Such clinics can give you advice on home dental hygiene techniques and will monitor your progress. They will also provide support if your dog has to undergo a dental procedure such as a scale-and-polish.

▲ **Scanning a microchip**
Checking that the microchip can be identified by a scanner is very important. Remember to keep the contact information registered against the chip number up to date.

Weight clinic

If your dog's weight is recorded at a regular clinic, any changes will be identified at an early stage. Unwanted weight gain may not be readily apparent from your dog's physical appearance, so the sooner the problem is picked up the less the dog will have to lose to return to his ideal body weight. It is equally important to pick up unintentional weight loss, which may occur in an active dog who is simply not eating enough to meet his energy requirements, but could also be warning of a health problem. Many dogs become so used to being weighed that they head straight for the scales when they come through the practice door.

Signs of ill health

Contact your veterinary practice for advice if you have any concerns about your dog, however trivial you think they might sound. If your worries prove to be unfounded then your mind will have been put at rest.

Recognizing a problem

Any change in your dog may be a warning of ill health. The most trivial sign, such as a droopy eyelid, should not be dismissed as it could be significant. Your dog may have an internal problem such as a stomach upset, an external problem affecting the coat and skin, or a combination of the two. You may notice only vague signs, such as sleeping more or exercising less readily, or something obviously wrong, such as the dog limping, or shaking his head because a grass awn is trapped in his ear.

Many common disorders are minor and easily treated, especially if they are recognized early. Always speak to your vet before attempting any home

◄ **Recognizing the warning signs**
It is helpful to understand what is normal in your dog. You will then be able to recognize anything unusual, such as lack of interest in food or exercise, that may be due to ill health.

Signs of a problem include:

- Lethargy, tiring unexpectedly on a walk
- Altered breathing pattern or an abnormal sound during respiration
- Coughing or sneezing
- Open wound
- Swelling or unusual bump
- Blood: from a wound; passed in urine (which will appear pink or contain blood clots); in faeces or vomit
- Limping or stiffness
- Unintentional weight loss
- Weight gain, particularly if the dog has developed a distended abdomen

- Reduced appetite or refusing food altogether
- Voracious appetite, or a change in what the dog will eat
- Vomiting, or regurgitation of food shortly after eating
- Diarrhoea or difficulty passing a motion
- Crying with pain when passing faeces or urine
- Itchiness: rubbing at mouth, eyes, or ears; dragging rear along the ground ("scooting") or washing excessively at that area; or all-over bodily itching

- Abnormal discharge: from any orifice (such as the mouth, nose, ear, vulva, prepuce, or anus) from which there is not usually a discharge, or because the normal smell, colour, or consistency has altered
- Coat changes: dull with a greasy texture, or excessively dry; debris in the coat such as flea dirts, actual fleas, scabs, or scales
- Excessive hair-loss resulting in areas of baldness
- Change in coat colour (may occur so gradually that it is noticed only when compared with an old photo)

treatment. What might seem an appropriate course of action for humans could be harmful to a dog. It may be sufficient to act on advice given by your vet practice over the telephone, although often the vet will need to examine your dog to be certain of how to proceed.

After taking a dog's history and examining him fully, the vet may still need to perform further investigations such as blood tests and imaging. Sometimes, a dog may be diagnosed with a serious disorder that needs hospitalization and even surgery, followed by a long convalescence – but, fortunately, common things really are common. An itchy dog is more likely to have fleas than an obscure problem with his nervous system.

Life-long health

In the following pages, there is an overview of some common canine disorders, together with advice on caring for a sick dog and coping with the special problems of elderly dogs. Remember, both you and your vet are aiming for your dog to lead as long and healthy a life as possible. If you need more advice or information, your vet will be ready to help.

What is abnormal thirst?

A dog spending more time than usual at his water bowl or a source of water outside, such as a pond or bucket, may have an abnormal thirst (p.112). If he uses a bowl then measure the volume of water he drinks over a 24-hour period by emptying all his bowls and recording how much you add (in millilitres); 24 hours later, measure how much is left and subtract that from the total. Divide that figure by your dog's body weight in kilogrammes – if it is around 50 then your dog's thirst is normal, but contact your vet if it is 90 or more.

"Any change in your dog may be a warning of ill health. The most trivial sign should not be dismissed as it could be significant."

▼ **Arriving at a diagnosis**
Many common disorders, for example ear mites, are simple for a vet to diagnose, and can be easily remedied. If there is no simple explanation of a problem, your vet will work through causes in order of likelihood.

Inherited disorders

An inherited disorder is one that is handed on from one generation to the next. Such disorders appear more often in pedigree dogs and may be breed-specific. Some common examples are described below.

The risk of disease

Smaller gene pools and widespread inbreeding in the past have made pedigree dogs more likely than crossbreeds to be affected by inherited disorders. However, although crossbred dogs may be at reduced risk they still have a chance of inheriting disease-causing genes from either parent.

Hip and elbow dysplasia

These two conditions occur mainly in medium-sized and large breeds. In dysplasia, structural defects either of the hip or the elbow cause a joint to become unstable, resulting in pain and lameness. Diagnosis is based on the dog's history, together with joint manipulation and radiography.

Treatment may consist of pain relief, reduced exercise, and maintaining ideal body weight. Various surgical options are also available, including total hip replacement for hip dysplasia. After a set age (generally more than one year old) susceptible breeds can be screened for hip and elbow dysplasia.

Aortic stenosis

A congenital defect, present from birth, aortic stenosis is a narrowing of the aortic valve in the heart. There may be no signs, the disorder being detected as a murmur when a vet listens to the heart with a stethoscope at a puppy check. It may be investigated further (with radiography, ultrasound, and ECG) or simply monitored, as only a few dogs can be treated surgically. Some dogs with aortic stenosis go on to develop congestive heart failure.

Blood clotting disorders

The most common inherited clotting disorder (in both dogs and humans) is haemophilia, in which lack of an essential factor for blood clotting results in recurrent bleeding. The faulty gene responsible is passed on by affected males to their female offspring, who remain unaffected

▶ **Radiograph of hip**
Screening is advisable before using a dog for breeding when hip dysplasia is known to occur in the breed. This involves submitting a radiograph of the dog's hips for scoring.

Hip scoring

The hips are radiographed with the dog lying on his back, hindlegs extended straight out. For best results, the dog may be given sedation to keep him in the right position. Each hip joint is given a score for six factors, covering conditions from normal to severe. This gives a maximum score of 53 for each hip – the ideal is for as low a score as possible. Adding the two scores together gives a total. When selections are being made for breeding purposes, the ideal is to choose a dog whose total score is less than the current average total for that breed.

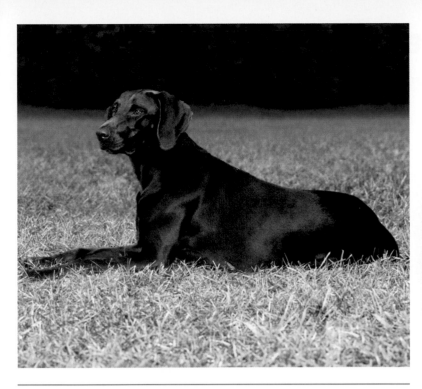

▼ **Collie eye anomaly (CEA)**
Collies such as the Australian Shepherd must be checked as puppies for CEA, because early signs can be masked as the dog matures.

"Screening is important. The advent of DNA screening has improved the chances of detecting many inherited diseases."

themselves but can be carriers of the gene. Haemophilia occurs in both pedigree and crossbred dogs.

A similar inherited bleeding disorder is Von Willebrand's disease, which can affect either sex. Many breeds can be affected, including the Dobermann and German Shepherd; DNA tests are available for some breeds.

Eye problems

Dogs can be affected by several inherited eye conditions, including some that are easily visible, such as entropion (p.98), and others that need internal examination of the eye using specialized equipment. An eye disease that can occur in any breed and also in crossbred dogs is progressive retinal atrophy (PRA). In

this disorder, there is degeneration of the retina – the layer of light-sensitive cells at the back of the eye – leading to loss of vision. An owner may become aware of PRA only when a dog has difficulties in seeing, which at first may be only at night.

PRA is diagnosed from examining the retina with an ophthalmoscope, and the vet may recommend more specialized investigations. There is no treatment and loss of vision is permanent. DNA screening is available for some breeds.

Various breeds of collie (Rough, Smooth, and Border Collies, Shetland Sheepdog, and Australian Shepherd) and some other breeds are affected by a disorder known as collie eye anomaly (CEA), in which there are abnormalities in the

choroid, a layer of tissue at the back of the eye. CEA can be detected from birth, so pups are examined before they are three months old. The mildest form of CEA has little effect on sight, but the most severe form can cause blindness. DNA screening is available.

Screening for disease

Routine screening is important in reducing the incidence of inherited diseases. For hip and elbow dysplasia, dogs are screened by having radiographs taken (see box, left). Eye conditions such as PRA and CEA once relied on examination and certification; however, the advent of DNA screening has improved the chances of detecting both these and many other inherited diseases.

Musculoskeletal disorders

Just like us, dogs are susceptible to minor strains and sprains, which usually resolve with rest. Sometimes a problem is more serious, so seek veterinary advice if your dog is persistently lame or unwilling to exercise.

Signs of a problem

- Limping (head lifted as lame forelimb lands on ground)
- Stiffness after resting
- Unwillingness to exercise; hanging back whilst on walk
- Reluctance to climb stairs or to jump into car
- Pain, swelling, and heat in joint
- Ataxia (loss of coordination) and paralysis
- Sudden halt during activity (and perhaps holding up back paw)

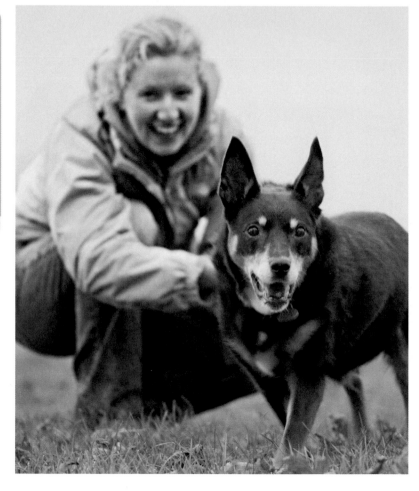

▲ **Elderly but active**
It is important to keep your senior dog's limbs moving, but he is likely to enjoy two or three short daily walks more than one tiring hike.

Arthritis

If a joint is unstable due to an injury, or to a skeletal abnormality such as hip dysplasia, arthritis may develop as a dog ages. This disease is associated with damage and inflammation that restrict joint movement and cause pain. Normal wear and tear can also lead to arthritis, especially if a dog has led a very active life or is overweight.

To investigate and diagnose an arthritic joint, your vet will palpate and manipulate the area, looking for swelling, heat, and abnormal movement, and may want to watch your dog move as you trot him up. Further investigation may be needed, such as radiography or withdrawal of a small sample of fluid from the joint for testing. MRI scanning is also increasingly used.

As well as pain relief with non-steroidal anti-inflammatory drugs, other ways of managing arthritis include weight control, changing your dog's exercise regime (taking him for more frequent but shorter walks), acupuncture, non-weight-bearing exercise such as swimming (hydrotherapy), and physiotherapy. Glucosamine, chondroitin, hyaluronic acid, and omega-3 fatty acids may also help, either taken as dietary supplements or included within the formulation of certain foods.

Panosteitis

In young, still-developing dogs, a bone disease called panosteitis can affect bone growth, causing lameness in different limbs at different times. This condition is especially common in larger breeds such as the German Shepherd and Labrador Retriever.

▲ Problems with stairs
If your dog has back pain, the prospect of going up a flight of stairs can be as daunting to him as climbing a mountain.

Panosteitis is confirmed by radiography and treated with rest and pain relief. The problem is usually temporary.

Prolapsed disc

A dog who is suddenly reluctant to go up stairs or jump into the car may have temporary neck or back pain, which improves with rest and anti-inflammatory drugs. A more serious problem, seen especially in long-backed breeds such as the Bassett Hound and Dachshund, is prolapse of one or more intervertebral discs. Symptoms may include pain, weakness, or paralysis of the hindlimbs – and the forelimbs if the prolapse is in the neck – and loss of sensation below the area of the affected disc. Strict rest and pain relief may be enough for recovery, but surgery, after radiography and MRI to pinpoint the problem, may be needed. If bladder and bowel control are lost the outlook is poor.

Hindleg disorders

It is common to see a dog, particularly a small breed such as a West Highland White or Yorkshire Terrier, trotting along and then skipping while carrying one backleg off the ground for a few steps before going on all four paws again. He probably has an intermittently slipping kneecap (luxating patella), commonly caused by the groove housing the kneecap being too shallow. The problem can be corrected surgically, but this is usually only necessary in a big dog, as little dogs cope very well. Another common hindleg problem is rupture of the cranial cruciate ligament, one of the stabilizing ligaments within the knee joint. This is often associated with an active dog who dashes off after a ball only to stop suddenly, holding up a back paw. The Golden Retriever and German Shepherd are among the breeds that seem to be prone. Surgery offers the best chance of recovery. For small dogs, pain relief and strict rest for several weeks may work.

▲ Restricted exercise
If your dog's exercise must be restricted after a joint injury, keep him on a lead to prevent possibly harmful bursts of over-activity.

Avoiding overload

Keeping your dog's weight at the correct level for his size and breed is one of the most important things you can do to help prevent joint problems. Obesity is not only detrimental to your dog's general health, it also overloads his joints, increasing the risk of irreversible and painful disorders such as arthritis.

Coat and skin disorders

A dog's coat and skin are easy to see, so problems with them are very common reasons for a trip to the vet. Do not ignore constant scratching or licking, which can turn a minor disorder into something more serious.

Allergy and infection

Dogs that are allergic to fleas, substances such as pollen, or certain foods often react with itchiness. Allergic skin disease, especially if it causes constant scratching, can lead to recurrent skin infections needing long courses of antibiotics. It is important to try to identify the triggers of an allergy, as it may be possible to avoid the problem (by changing to a hypoallergenic diet, for example), or to treat it with a desensitizing vaccine course. Antihistamines can help limit itchiness, but some dogs need low-dose corticosteroids.

Acute moist dermatitis

Also known as a hot spot, this is a sticky area of infected oozy, often smelly skin which the dog exacerbates by repeatedly licking and scratching. The original cause may have been an insect sting. Treatment is aimed at thoroughly cleansing the area and preventing further self-harm, together with antibiotics and bathing twice daily with a teaspoonful of salt in half a litre of warm water.

Anal furunculosis

If your dog shows extreme pain when passing faeces, he may have a serious, deep-seated condition in the tissues around the anus known as anal furunculosis. The disorder may be accompanied by colitis or irritable bowel syndrome. Looking under the tail reveals a raw, malodorous area of ulceration. The current approach is drug treatment to suppress the immune response that causes the problem, with surgery if the area does not heal fully. However, unfortunately treatment is not always successful.

▲ **Itchy skin**
Fleas are the most common cause of skin irritation but if fine-combing fails to detect them, ask your vet to check your dog for other possible problems.

Sebaceous adenitis

This autoimmune disorder targets the hair follicles, especially the glands within them that produce sebum, the oily substance that protects and waterproofs the hair and skin. Symptoms include alopecia (hair loss), scaling of the skin, and sometimes intense itching. Recurrent secondary bacterial skin infections can be a complication. Treatment relies on shampoos, oil baths, dietary supplements, and antibiotics.

Ringworm

A highly contagious fungal skin infection, ringworm can be transmitted to humans. The disease causes scaling and crusting of the skin, and hair loss. It is usually diagnosed by checking the area with a fluorescent lamp or placing hairs on a culture medium and watching for signs of fungal growth. Other pets should be tested as well. Treatment includes shampoos, creams, and oral drugs. The fungal spores can persist for months, so you should destroy all your dog's grooming tools, collars, leads, and bedding, and vigorously vacuum your house and car.

Skin growths

Growths such as cysts, warts, and tumours may be seen or felt in your dog's skin. Always have lumps investigated, as early diagnosis and treatment could be vital. Your vet may take a few cells or a small section of the mass for diagnosis before making a plan for action.

Persistent licking
Allowing a dog to lick at an itchy area, perhaps after an insect sting, can lead to infection and a worse problem to manage. On the lower leg, covering the area with a sock may be enough to break the cycle.

Eye disorders

Always check that your dog's eyes are open and bright. Many eye problems quickly become obvious, but some disorders affecting the inside of the eye may not be suspected until the dog's sight is affected.

Conjunctivitis

Unlike the highly infectious eye disorder that affects people, conjunctivitis in dogs simply means inflammation of the conjunctiva, the layer covering the front of the eyeball. The most apparent sign is reddening inside the lower eyelid. There may be a discharge, initially clear but becoming white or green if an infection develops. Your dog may blink rapidly because of pain. The inflammation is sometimes due to an allergy to pollen, but the commonest causes of conjunctivitis in one eye are foreign bodies, such as a grass awn or a speck of grit.

Your vet may numb the front of the eye with local anaesthetic drops to make an examination. Fluorescein dye applied to the eye may reveal an injury to the cornea such as a scratch. There may be a film over the eye due to an inflamed cornea, as well as conjunctivitis. Prompt attention is needed as the iris can be affected too, with painful spasm of the pupil. Your dog may be prescribed pain relief and oral antibiotics as well as eye drops, and will need careful monitoring. For allergy-related conjunctivitis, steroid eye drops help to reduce the inflammation. Your dog may need an Elizabethan collar to stop him rubbing his eye.

Entropion and ectropion

The eyelids have a protective role but if they roll inwards, a condition called entropion, the eyelashes rub against the front of the eye causing conjunctivitis and corneal ulceration. Entropion is usually congenital, but can develop after injury or as a result of chronic conjunctivitis. The dog will blink more often and rub at his eyes, resulting in infection and a thick discharge. Entropion is corrected by surgery, although there is a risk of

◄ **Vet check**
Eye problems need prompt attention from a vet. Do not ignore signs such as a discharge or a dog pawing at his eyes because of irritation.

◄ **Eye problems in the Shar Pei**
Entropion, a painful inrolling of the eyelids, is common in the Shar Pei, usually developing in very young puppies. Both upper and lower eyelids may be affected.

over-correction and ectropion, an outward rolling of the eyelid that exposes the eye to potential injury. Ectropion can also occur naturally, congenitally, or in old age. Usually, only extreme cases are corrected. Some breeds, such as the English Bulldog and Cocker Spaniel, are prone to a combination of entropion and ectropion.

Cataract

In this disorder, the transparent lens of the eye, which directs light to the retina, becomes opaque, impairing sight. Cataracts can be hereditary or may form in response to retinal disease, glaucoma, or diabetes (p.132). Senile cataracts may develop in old dogs. Cataracts can be removed surgically, usually only if the retina is intact so that the dog will see afterwards.

Glaucoma

Raised pressure within the eyeball, known as glaucoma, causes pain and ultimately loss of vision. The condition can be treated but needs early diagnosis to avoid blindness. Glaucoma is an inherited problem in some breeds, including the Beagle and Bassett Hound.

Dry eye

Lack of tear production to lubricate the eyes results in dryness and a thick discharge due to infection. Dry eye is diagnosed by a painless test and treated with eye drops or surgery. It is an inherited problem in some breeds, for example, the West Highland White Terrier.

Horner's syndrome

This is a classic set of signs, usually affecting one eye only, that include a sunken eyeball, drooping of the upper eyelid, prominence of the third eyelid at the inner corner of the eye, and constriction of the pupil. Often, the cause is unknown and the condition resolves over a few weeks, but your dog should be examined by a vet for possible underlying health problems.

Applying eye drops

Supporting your dog's head, gently pull down on the lower eyelid and raise the upper lid.

Hold the dropper between your thumb and forefinger and squeeze the drops onto the front of the eye.

After applying the drops, gently hold your dog's eyelids closed for a few seconds.

Ear disorders

The most common ear problems in dogs are infections, mites, and foreign bodies in the ear canal; some breeds are prone to deafness. See your vet promptly if your dog is showing any signs of an ear infection.

Signs of a problem

- Shaking head, yelping
- Rubbing at one ear
- Rubbing at both ears (can be sign of an allergy)
- Smelly ear or ears
- Pain when ear is touched
- Pain while eating
- Deafness
- Swollen ear flap (aural haematoma)
- Head tilt, loss of balance, nausea (can be signs of middle or inner ear disease)

Aural haematoma

Bleeding can sometimes occur inside a dog's ear flap, causing a swelling known as an aural haematoma. This condition may occur in a dog that constantly flicks his head about or scratches his ear. Often, the haematoma is accompanied by infection in the outer ear canal. A vet may be able to reduce the swelling by draining the blood through a needle and injecting a corticosteroid. Some dogs can tolerate this procedure without sedation. Surgery is also an option. Left untreated, the ear flap will shrink and crinkle.

Outer ear problems

If you see your dog rubbing at his ear, he may be troubled by an allergy, ear mites, or an infection. Another common problem is a sharp grass awn lodged in the outer ear canal; this is extremely painful and your dog will probably react by vigorously shaking his head and yelping.

To look down the full length of the outer canal to the ear drum, your vet will use a viewing instrument called an auroscope. This examination can be painful for your dog and he may have to be sedated first.

◄ **Hazard in the grass**
A dog that suddenly starts pawing at an ear, shaking his head, and squealing after running outdoors is likely to have picked up a grass awn in the outer ear canal. Removal may have to be done under sedation or general anaesthetic.

▼ **Binding an ear**
A cut ear flap will bleed profusely from even a small nick. The wound should be treated and the ear bandaged to the head to prevent the dog flicking it and causing fresh bleeding.

Ear mites are treated with ear drops or spot-on products that are applied directly to the skin on the back of the neck. Infections are initially treated with antibiotic ear drops, but if this fails the vet will take a swab for microscopic examination and testing for drug sensitivity. The infected ear may be flushed under general anaesthetic; occasionally, surgery is necessary. Grass awns may be removed under general anaesthetic.

Middle and inner ear

Infections of the outer ear sometimes spread to the middle part of the ear. Another cause of middle ear infection is penetration of the ear drum by a foreign body. Middle and inner ear infections can also be caused by an adverse reaction to ear drops used to treat outer ear problems. The signs of infection include pain on opening the mouth, lethargy, and discharge. Other common signs are loss of balance, head tilting, and vomiting.

In both middle and inner ear disease, early diagnosis – often with imaging such as radiography and MRI – and treatment are vital.

Deafness

Many older dogs are affected by age-related deafness and are hard to wake or fail to come when you call – but you should suspect selective deafness if your senior reacts promptly to the rattle of a food bowl.

Congenital deafness is often hereditary and possibly linked to coat colour; white-coated breeds, such as the English Bull Terrier and the Dalmatian, are particularly susceptible. A profoundly deaf puppy can be identified readily, as he responds to sounds differently from his littermates.

Your dog's hearing can be assessed using the Brainstem Auditory Evoked Response test (BAER) which detects electrical activity in the inner ear and aural pathways of the brain. It is painless and can be performed on puppies without distressing them, although older dogs may need sedation.

"In middle and inner ear disease, early diagnosis and treatment are vital."

Applying ear drops

Shake the bottle if the ear drops are in suspension, and gently pull back the ear flap to expose the ear canal.

Still holding back the ear flap, squirt the recommended number of drops into the ear canal.

Gently massage the ear to help the drops to penetrate. Afterwards, give your dog plenty of praise and a treat.

Mouth and tooth disorders

We should look after our dogs' teeth and gums, just as we do our own, to minimize the chances of disease. Regular dental checks, which can be carried out at a veterinary practice, are important to a dog's health.

Signs of a problem

- Bad breath (halitosis)
- Discolouration of teeth
- Yellow deposit of calcified plaque on teeth
- Swelling on side of face (tooth root abscess)
- Grey discharge at gum line (pus from tooth root abscess)
- Difficulty eating, perhaps yelping with pain (rotten or broken tooth, something stuck across roof of mouth or between the teeth)
- Drooling saliva, pus, or blood
- Gum proliferation or growth

Plaque and hygiene

In a healthy mouth, a dog's teeth are white and his gums a pale pink. Ideally, the teeth should be brushed regularly at home to remove plaque, a soft colourless substance that accumulates on the teeth after eating. With time, plaque hardens as yellow tartar or calculus, which needs to be removed with an ultrasonic scaler under general anaesthetic.

Without intervention, plaque build-up can lead to gum disease and teeth may ultimately loosen and fall out. If infection sets in, you may see pus at the gum line, or a swelling on the cheek caused by a tooth root abscess. Your dog may have smelly breath or drool blood-tinged saliva; he may have trouble eating, perhaps pawing at his mouth because of pain and refusing hard biscuits and dried foods. If your dog's mouth is very painful, he may have to be anaesthetized for the vet to find out exactly what is going on.

Teeth which cannot be saved will be

▼ **Dental check-up**
Your vet will look at your dog's teeth and mouth as part of a general examination, and may recommend that you book a dental clinic appointment for a more specific check.

▲ Retained teeth
Here, the puppy upper canine can be seen sitting behind (to the left), of the adult tooth, causing a potential food trap.

► Undershot jaw
The lower jaw jutting out in front of the upper jaw is a feature of some breeds, such as this Bulldog, contributing to the shape of the face.

extracted. Advanced dental procedures such as root canal treatment may be possible. After extractions, your dog will be discharged with antibiotics and pain relief. As plaque starts accumulating as soon as your dog starts eating again, vigilant home care is vital, together with regular dental check-ups.

Retained puppy teeth

Sometimes the puppy teeth do not fall out when the adult versions break through. Having both sets can crowd the other teeth and create food traps, leading to infection. Your vet will probably recommend removal of any unwanted puppy teeth (most conveniently, this could be done when your puppy is anaesthetized to be neutered).

Malocclusions

If a dog's jaws are not aligned correctly, the teeth do not pass each other normally, a condition described as a malocclusion or, more commonly, an overshot or undershot jaw. This can be a recognized feature of some breeds, but is regarded as a fault in others. Malocclusion carries

an increased risk of periodontal disease (that is, in the tissues surrounding the teeth) so careful dental hygiene, including tooth brushing, is very important. Your vet will look for misaligned teeth at your puppy's first check. Malocclusion can occasionally occur after an accident such as a fall onto the face.

Foreign objects

Pieces of wood, chews, and bones can all become wedged across the roof of the mouth or between teeth. Sedation or general anaesthesia may be needed to examine the mouth, remove the foreign object, and treat any injuries caused.

Jaw drop

This curious condition is characterized by a sudden inability to close the mouth, together with excessive salivation and difficulty swallowing. Despite appearances, it is not painful. Fortunately, jaw drop usually self-cures over several days; the main concern is to ensure that your dog takes in enough food and water.

Jaw pain

Inflammation can sometimes develop in the muscles used for chewing, making it painful for a dog to eat. The dog may not be able to close his mouth fully and will drool saliva, looking as though he might have jaw drop. Jaw pain is seen in all breeds but especially the German Shepherd dog. The condition usually responds to a course of high-dose corticosteroids.

Care after dental treatment

When you collect your dog from the vet after a dental procedure, he may be drooling, which is common after a general anaesthetic. Let him settle at home before you feed him. Unless he was discharged with a prescription diet, offer a small amount of bland home-cooked food such as chicken and rice. Continue with this for a few days, especially if he had extractions, weaning him back to his usual diet once his mouth has healed.

Respiratory disorders

It is easy to spot if your dog has a respiratory problem. Normally, a dog breathes through his mouth and pants only when he is hot or after exertion. If the pattern changes, or he develops a cough, consult your vet.

Signs of a problem

- Nasal discharge (on one or both sides – watery, white-green, or bloody)
- Sneezing or honking (reverse sneezing)
- Painful, one-sided facial swelling, which may affect the eye on that side
- Noisy breathing
- Difficulty breathing, with increased chest movements
- Poor exercise tolerance
- Cough
- Bluish tinge to gums (indicating shortage of oxygen in blood, due to reduced lung function)

Inhaled foreign body

Sniffing is what dogs do, and if they inhale an object they usually expel it by sneezing. However, something like a grass awn in a nostril can be on a one-way journey. Despite paroxysms of sneezing, the awn may move through the nasal chamber, scratching the delicate lining. The first sign of trouble may be a discharge, initially colourless but becoming thick and white or green as bacteria move in. It is therefore important to remove the awn as soon as possible. The vet may be able to see a foreign body through an auroscope inserted into the nostril; otherwise, under general anaesthetic, the object may be located through a fine endoscope passed down the dog's nose, and then removed.

▲ Close contact
Airborne infections spread rapidly between dogs housed in close proximity, either in kennels or within a household.

Kennel cough

This highly contagious disorder is usually a viral infection, although it can also be caused by Bordetella bronchiseptica, a common secondary bacterial invader. Kennel cough spreads readily between dogs, especially if they are housed together, such as in kennels and at dog shows; animals in a multi-dog household are also vulnerable.

The dog may seem well, apart from coughing up white frothy sputum, or he may be lethargic with a fever. For viral infections, treatment is aimed at relieving illness and the dog should be isolated until coughing stops, to prevent the spread of infection. Antibiotics are used only for bacterial infections.

Honking

In some dogs the soft palate (the flexible tissue at the back of the mouth) is longer than normal, which can result in it being inhaled into the airway. When this happens, the dog makes a characteristic honking sound as he tries to catch his breath until the airway clears. Excitement and exertion are common triggers, as is an allergic reaction to pollen. Corrective surgery may be needed if honking is a persistent problem.

Laryngeal paralysis

This disorder of the larynx (voicebox) occurs from middle age onwards in any type of dog but often in Labradors and Golden Retrievers. There is noisy breathing, often with a hoarse cough,

an altered bark, reduced ability to exercise, and sometimes severe difficulty breathing. Laryngeal paralysis can develop for no apparent reason, but may occur if a neck or chest injury causes damage to the nerves controlling the larynx, and is sometimes an effect of an underactive thyroid.

Any underlying cause should be treated if possible. Corticosteroids can sometimes improve the problem. Surgery to reduce breathing difficulties is high risk.

Lung disorders

Diseases of the lungs can include bronchitis (especially in older dogs), pneumonia, tumours, and fluid build-up due to heart failure. Such

problems restrict lung function, causing the dog to breathe more rapidly and noisily and/or develop a cough. Radiography is often used to diagnose lung disorders and can sometimes be carried out without sedation, an important factor if a dog is having difficulty breathing. If it is necessary to examine the airway directly, for example if a trapped foreign body is suspected, then an endoscope may be passed down under general anaesthetic.

Many lung disorders respond to drug treatment. It may be possible to surgically remove a single lung tumour, but multiple secondary growths, usually a sign of advanced cancer, are likely to be inoperable.

Preventing the spread of respiratory disease

The spread of diseases passed on by infected droplets can be prevented by rapidly isolating a dog who is coughing or is known to have been in contact with a coughing dog. Vaccination may provide some protection against kennel cough, depending on the specific bacteria or virus.

Heart and blood disorders

A healthy heart and circulation are essential to life. If a dog has a heart or blood disorder, early diagnosis is vital. Treatment should include good home management and regular monitoring; surgery may be an option.

Signs of a problem

- Cough
- Laboured breathing
- Blue (cyanotic) gums and tongue
- Fatigue and lethargy
- Poor exercise tolerance, tiring easily
- Weight loss
- Reduced appetite and increased thirst
- Bloated abdomen
- Fainting (syncope)
- In anaemia: pale gums, or yellowing of gums and whites of eyes, fatigue, black faeces, blood in urine.

▲ **Listening to the heart**
Whilst listening to a dog's heart through a stethoscope, the vet will pick up any abnormal sounds that could indicate a problem.

Congenital heart defect

Sometimes a puppy's heart does not develop normally in the womb, leading to congenital defects (present from birth). One of the most common of such disorders is called patent ductus arteriosus (PDA). Before a puppy is born, its blood bypasses the lungs through a channel (called the ductus arteriosus) running between the pulmonary artery and the aorta. In PDA, the channel does not close as it should soon after birth, and normal circulation is disrupted. The defect is heard through a stethoscope as a murmur, or blurring of the clear "lub-dub" sounds of a normal heartbeat. PDA is confirmed with radiography, ultrasound scanning, and ECG; in most cases the problem can be surgically corrected.

Heart valve defects also give rise to murmurs. It is not always possible to correct such defects surgically, and congestive heart failure (below) may develop later.

Congestive heart failure

In this disorder, the heart fails to pump efficiently. A common cause of congestive heart failure in old dogs is a diseased heart valve. Your vet may detect a murmur before a problem becomes apparent, which might not happen in your dog's lifetime. Early signs of congestive heart failure are typically a reduced ability to exercise, with panting and breathlessness. In the later stages, a cough develops, often at night and on rising in the morning, there is weight loss, and the dog has a reduced appetite but an increased thirst. His abdomen may swell with fluid, making him look pot-bellied. Diagnostic tests for congestive heart failure include radiography, ultrasound scan,

ECG, and blood tests. Treatment includes drugs, a prescription diet, and weight management, and surgery for an underlying cause may be possible.

Dilated cardiomyopathy

This condition especially affects the Boxer, Dobermann, and Great Dane. The heart is unable to contract properly and there may be a disordered heart rhythm, resulting in weakness, difficulty breathing, a cough, fainting, loss of appetite, and weight loss.

Radiography, ultrasound, and ECG confirm the diagnosis. Treatment is aimed at improving quality of life, as the outlook is, sadly, poor.

Blood abnormalities

Dogs can be affected by various blood disorders, one of the most common of which is anaemia. In this condition, the blood has a reduced oxygen-carrying capacity because of either insufficient red blood cells or a low concentration of the oxygen-carrying pigment haemoglobin. Types of anaemia include an immune system disorder called immune-mediated haemolytic anaemia (p.119), and iron-deficiency anaemia, which could be caused, for example, by bleeding from a stomach ulcer, and is indicated by a dog passing dark faeces. Treatment of anaemia depends on the underlying cause.

Clotting disorders are often inherited (pp.92–3), but can be an effect of eating rat poison (p.142).

Home care for your dog

The key to caring for a dog with a heart condition is to let him take life at his own pace, avoiding undue stress – which may mean leading a quieter life yourself. Exercise should be short and gentle, perhaps in the garden, so that he can stop and rest when he wants. He will need to avoid weight gain, which will put additional stress on his heart. Your vet may recommend a specific prescription diet for dogs with heart disease.

▲ Breed at risk
The Great Dane is a breed prone to dilated cardiomyopathy. Early diagnosis is important so that drug treatment can be started before the disease has become too advanced.

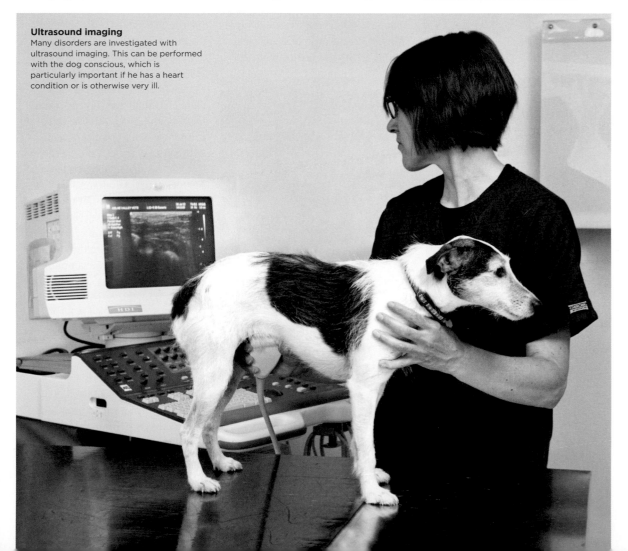

Ultrasound imaging
Many disorders are investigated with ultrasound imaging. This can be performed with the dog conscious, which is particularly important if he has a heart condition or is otherwise very ill.

Digestive disorders

Minor stomach upsets are common in dogs, who are always ready to grab forbidden food. Having a good gag reflex, they usually vomit up anything unsuitable. Occasionally, more serious gastric problems can arise.

Signs of a problem:

- Vomiting or regurgitation
- Constipation (as a result of, for example, eating bones)
- Diarrhoea (frequently passing large volumes of loose faeces)
- Colitis (straining to pass loose faeces containing mucus and blood)
- Altered stools (either in colour, frequency, or consistency)
- Weight loss

Obstruction

A brief bout of vomiting usually means a short-lived stomach upset. Repeated vomiting may indicate a foreign body, such as a bone or a child's toy, blocking the stomach or intestine. If the object is in the stomach, the dog can appear quite normal; a dog with an intestinal obstruction looks "tucked up", standing crouched over a painful abdomen. This condition needs rapid investigation. A small foreign object may be retrieved from the stomach via an endoscope passed down the throat. Otherwise, surgery is needed. During recovery, the dog needs light food, such as chicken with boiled rice.

Obstruction due to "bloat" is a medical and surgical emergency. In this condition, gas accumulates in the stomach causing bloating (gastric dilatation) and sometimes twisting of the stomach (volvulus). Large deep-chested breeds like the Great Dane are particularly prone to this disorder. Your dog should be seen by a vet as soon as possible if he is restless, retching, and drooling, especially after eating, and has a distended abdomen. To help avoid bloat, your dog should rest, and avoid drinking much water for an hour either side of eating. Feeding several small meals throughout the day also helps ease the symptoms.

Constipation is another form of obstruction, which may cause a dog to lose his appetite and even vomit. Treatment depends on the underlying cause (for example, eating bones) and the severity of the constipation. If laxatives are ineffective, an enema will be given under general anaesthetic.

Diarrhoea

Sudden change in diet is a very common cause of diarrhoea in dogs. Introduce any new food to your dog by mixing it with his usual meals in

◄ **Risk of obstruction**
If your dog swallows a large object such as a piece of wood or a stone, or even something unusual like a sock or child's toy, it may lodge in the stomach or intestines, causing vomiting.

▲ Taking time to recover
Your dog will feel lethargic and sleep more than usual while recovering from a stomach upset. Encourage him to drink frequent small amounts of rehydration fluid or cool boiled water and avoid strenuous exercise until he is well.

▼ Light meals
When a dog is recovering from a digestive disorder, he needs small frequent meals once he can keep fluids down. Your vet may put him on a prescription diet, but otherwise offer him easily digested food, such as chicken.

ever-increasing proportions, giving the natural gut flora time to adjust.

Most adult dogs are lactose intolerant and will have diarrhoea if they drink cows' milk. Less common is intolerance to gluten, the protein found in wheat, which also causes diarrhoea and weight loss. Blood tests and diarrhoea clearing up on a trial gluten-free diet confirm the diagnosis.

Pancreatic problems

The pancreas produces important digestive enzymes but if it fails to produce enough the result will be a ravenous dog with diarrhoea and weight loss. Pancreatic function is checked by blood tests, and missing enzymes will be replaced with dietary supplements.

A more serious illness is inflammation of the pancreas (pancreatitis). A high-fat meal is a common trigger, such as eating

a fat ball left out for wild birds. Symptoms may be vague but can include intermittent vomiting and acute abdominal pain and swelling. Blood tests and an ultrasound scan confirm the diagnosis. Treatment includes pain relief, anti-nausea medication, and hospitalization for intravenous fluid therapy.

Dangers of dehydration

Small dogs and puppies in particular can become dehydrated and weak from recurrent vomiting and diarrhoea (gastroenteritis) within a matter of hours and, at worst, may need to be hospitalized and given fluids intravenously. If you are at all concerned about a dog or puppy with gastroenteritis, contact your vet as early as possible.

Reproductive disorders

Various problems can affect the reproductive organs of dogs, including infections and tumours. Neutering, which is often advised in the case of family pets, can reduce the risk of serious disorders in both sexes.

Normal seasons in bitches

If you have an un-neutered bitch, it is important to understand what happens during her normal reproductive cycle. A bitch can be expected to have her first season from six months of age, and she will then continue to come into season every 6–12 months, although there can be wide variations. She will lose a variable quantity of blood from the vulva, which may be missed if she is meticulous about washing. If you do not want her to be mated, you should isolate her whilst she is in season to avoid attracting every intact male in the area.

False pregnancy

This is a normal part of the bitch's reproductive cycle which happens a few weeks after her season is over. Often, a bitch shows signs of maternal behaviour, or nesting, when she takes toys and other objects into her bed. Her teats may become swollen and her mammary glands may start producing milk. False pregnancy can, however, also result in unpredictable behaviour and aggression, which may respond to drug treatment.

Mammary tumours

Tumours of the mammary glands often develop around the time a bitch is in season, under the influence of the sex hormones, but they can also arise independently of the reproductive cycle. Mammary tumours may be benign but if they are malignant they have the potential to spread to adjacent mammary glands and to the lungs. The likelihood of tumours developing is reduced by neutering before your bitch has had many seasons. Your vet will routinely

◄ **Taking an interest**
In a sexually mature dog, taking an interest in the opposite sex is natural. Neutering not only prevents unwanted behaviour but can lessen the risk of many reproductive disorders.

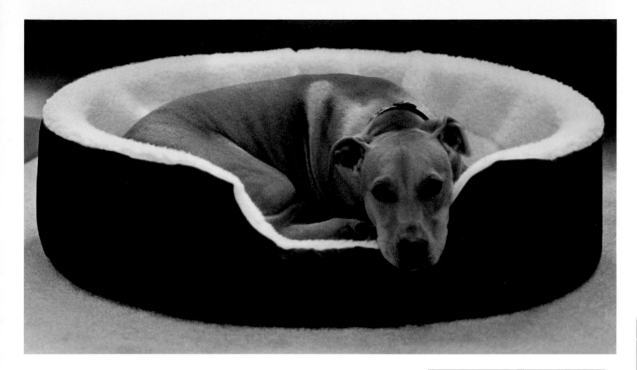

▲ Nesting instinct
It is quite normal for an unneutered bitch to experience regular false pregnancies. She may treat her bed as a nest, collecting up objects as though to mother them, and may sometimes become quite possessive about them.

run a hand along your bitch's belly, feeling the mammary glands for masses. Should you find a growth then contact your vet.

Womb infection

Infection of the womb, or pyometra, classically develops a few weeks after a bitch has been in season. You may notice that there is an unpleasant discharge from her vulva but little other illness apparent. Alternatively, your bitch may be very ill, running a fever, lacking appetite, vomiting, urinating frequently, and drinking excessively. She may have a tender, distended abdomen. The usual treatment for pyometra is neutering but the risk of complications is high because of the bitch being unwell. Sometimes, the infection clears up with a course of antibiotics but is

likely to return after the next season. Ideally, neutering should take place before then, whilst the bitch is fit and healthy.

Retained testicles

In male dogs, one testicle or both may be retained within the abdomen or in the groin rather than being in the scrotum. If a puppy has retained testicles, the vet will regularly check the scrotum until the testicles are fully descended. If this does not happen neutering will be advised because the condition carries an increased chance of testicular tumours.

Testicular tumour

In older dogs, there may be a noticeable disparity in the size of the testicles. The development of a testicular tumour will often make one testicle large and firm while the other shrinks down and becomes flabby. Treatment is to remove both testicles, but will not cure a tumour that has spread.

Neutering

If you do not intend to breed from your dog, he or she can be neutered before reaching sexual maturity. In bitches, neutering avoids such problems as womb infections and growths in the ovaries and womb. In male dogs, neutering prevents testicular growths, and is often advised for a young dog who starts to show inappropriate behaviour such as mounting people's legs and running off after bitches in season. The metabolism in dogs of either sex slows down after neutering, so aim for your pet to be at the correct body weight beforehand.

Urinary tract disorders

Problems in the urinary tract will rapidly affect your dog's general health and need fast diagnosis. Look out for any change in his normal intake of water and output of urine, as this could be an early warning sign.

Signs of a problem

- Squatting or cocking leg frequently but passing only a few spots of urine
- Frequently passing a large volume of urine (polyuria)
- Change in colour of urine from normal pale yellow
- Abdominal pain
- Increased thirst (polydipsia), drinking more than 100ml water per kilogramme body weight over a 24-hour period (easy to measure if your dog is the only household pet and not drinking from an outside water source such as a pond)

Cystitis

Bladder infections (cystitis) tend to be more common in bitches, because the female urethra, the tube that carries urine from the bladder, is shorter than in male dogs, making it easier for bacteria to enter the body. A dog with cystitis may repeatedly pass only a small amount of urine, which may contain blood and look pink. If you can collect a urine sample (see box, opposite) it will help diagnosis; otherwise, your vet may take a sample directly from the bladder. If infection is present, the vet will prescribe an appropriate antibiotic.

It is important to find any underlying cause for cystitis.

▶ **Excessive thirst**
If your dog spends a long time standing drinking over the water bowl, or repeatedly visiting it, then he may have an excessive thirst that could be linked to a bladder or kidney problem.

For example, glucose in the urine associated with diabetes mellitus can increase susceptibility to bladder infections. A less common cause of bladder infection is a growth in the bladder wall. This may be detected by your vet palpating your dog's bladder, or during a bladder scan.

Urinary stones

Cystitis may also be associated with the presence of crystals in the urine, which can be seen under a microscope. A further complication is that urinary crystals can form into stones in the bladder. Your vet may be able to feel the stones manually and they can also be picked up by radiography or an ultrasound scan. Some bladder stones can be dissolved with medication, but other types have to be removed surgically. Extracted stones are analysed in a laboratory to determine how to prevent further stones from forming.

If a stone passes from the bladder, a male dog's urethra may become blocked because it is a long and narrow tube (unlike a bitch's urethra, which is short and wide). This situation requires urgent veterinary attention. Not only is the condition extremely painful, but it prevents the passage of urine out of the bladder, leading to pressure backing up to the kidneys and damaging them.

> **"It is important to differentiate between a house-training lapse and incontinence."**

▲ Bladder infections are uncomfortable
Having cystitis is unpleasant and can make a normally active dog feel under the weather and disinterested in exercise.

Prostatic disease

The prostate, the sex gland lying around the urethra of the male dog, is prone to various disorders. Bacterial infection ascending from the urethra can cause swelling and inflammation of the prostate. Symptoms may include blood dripping from the penis, urinary incontinence or difficulty passing urine, abdominal pain, and straining to pass faeces. Infection is treated with antibiotics and castration. Swelling can also be caused by benign prostatic enlargement, which occurs in an un-neutered dog and is treated by castration. Rarely, prostate enlargement is due to a tumour, especially in castrated dogs.

Urinary incontinence

It is important to differentiate between a house-training lapse, when your dog consciously empties his bladder but just cannot get outside in time, and incontinence, where urine leaks out when your dog is relaxed or asleep. In a puppy, incontinence may be due to a congenital anatomical problem, for which surgical treatment may be possible. Some dogs may become incontinent after neutering, and some require long-term medication; incontinence in old age can also be controlled medically to some extent. Your vet will want to check that there is no underlying disease.

Urine testing

A useful specimen to take to the vet is a sample of the first urine your dog passes in the morning. Use a sealable container and be prepared to move quickly to catch the stream as your pet squats or cocks a leg. Your vet can provide a "collection kit" to make it easier.

Kidney disease

The kidneys – which filter wastes from the blood – are susceptible to infection and can be affected by some inherited diseases. Kidney failure is common in old dogs. Signs of disease include increased thirst and urination, with weight loss, poor appetite, and vomiting developing later. Urine and blood tests help identify the cause.

Nervous system disorders

The nervous system comprises the brain and spinal cord, and the nerve pathways that carry signals throughout the body. Disorders can occur in any part of this system, affecting the way a dog moves and behaves.

Juvenile epilepsy

Fits, or seizures, are caused by electrical disturbances in the brain and can occur in a dog at any age (pp.138–9). However, if a dog first starts fitting whilst he is young, then a disorder known as juvenile epilepsy is suspected. Blood is usually taken to rule out other causes for fits such as liver disease. If the blood results are normal, juvenile epilepsy tends to be the diagnosis, especially in a breed known to be prone to the disorder, such as the Beagle, Border Collie, German Shepherd, Golden and Labrador Retrievers, and Irish Setter. Anti-epileptic drugs will be needed for life.

Wobbler syndrome

Caused by a malformation of the neck bones putting pressure on the spinal cord, wobbler syndrome makes a dog move in an abnormal way, taking short steps with his front legs and wandering, wobbly steps with his back legs. He may also have neck pain. There are two forms of wobbler syndrome: one appears at an early age in giant breeds such as the Great Dane and gradually worsens; the other form occurs in the Dobermann, and does not appear until middle age. The diagnosis is confirmed by radiography and MRI. Treatment with corticosteroids may help and in some cases, surgery is advised.

Hydrocephalus

This is a congenital problem (present from birth) that occurs in the Chihuahua, Pekingese, and Boston Terrier among others. In hydrocephalus, the fluid that flows round the brain and spinal cord to protect them from injury, is

◄ **CT scanning**
Combining computer technology with X-rays, CT scanning detects abnormalities by producing images of the body in cross section, and is invaluable for investigating brain disorders.

► **Problems in the Chihuahua**
Syringomyelia, a brain disorder which affects a dog's gait and posture, is inherited in dome-headed breeds such as the Chihuahua.

▼ **Susceptible to fits**
The German Shepherd is one of several breeds known to be at risk of juvenile epilepsy. Drug treatment is used to manage the disorder.

prevented from draining away normally. The build-up of fluid leads to pressure inside the skull and the risk of brain damage. Severely affected puppies, which often do not survive long after birth, have a markedly domed skull, and fail to grow and develop like their littermates. Mild cases of hydrocephalus may not be recognized until a dog is older.

MRI or CT scanning, or possibly ultrasound imaging, will confirm the diagnosis. Drug treatment may reduce fluid production; it may also be possible to insert a shunt (tube) in the brain to drain excess fluid.

IVS

Often mistakenly called a stroke by owners, Ideopathic Vestibular Syndrome (IVS) usually occurs in old dogs, affecting the centre of balance within the inner ear. The dog suddenly develops a head tilt and may lose his balance. His eyes flick from

side to side as they try to stop the world from spinning. Some dogs are so badly affected that they are nauseous and vomit, and walk round in circles. IVS usually resolves on its own after a few days. Your vet may give a drug to reduce nausea if your dog cannot keep down food and water. A drug that promotes blood supply to the brain is available and can help to prevent the disease.

CDRM

This distressing disease – chronic degenerative radiculomyelopathy (CDRM) – affects the spinal cord. It causes a dog to gradually lose hindlimb co-ordination and movement, even though he is otherwise well and retains voluntary control over his bladder and bowels. Breeds in which CDRM occurs include the German Shepherd, Boxer, and Pembroke Corgi. There is no treatment, other than helping the dog to cope.

Syringomyelia

SM, as this disease is known, is characterized by head and neck pain that may be hard to localize. A dog may sleep with his head in a strange position, show pain on being picked up, or have difficulty going up stairs. The classic sign is for the dog to walk along kicking with a hindleg as if to scratch his ear. The commonest cause of SM is a structural defect in the brain that causes a misfit between brain size and the space in the skull. This is an inherited disorder in dome-headed breeds such as the Cavalier King Charles Spaniel, Chihuahua, and Griffon Bruxellois.

Definitive diagnosis requires an MRI scan, which is also used for screening. Treatment aims at pain control, with lifestyle changes such as feeding from a raised bowl and walking on the lead with a body harness rather than a collar. Surgery is also possible.

Hormonal disorders

Hormones are chemicals released into the bloodstream by various glands to carry messages to body tissues and organs. Most hormonal disorders occur through overproduction or underproduction of these chemicals.

Signs of a problem

■ Increased thirst (needing water bowl filled more often; drinking from ponds or puddles)
■ Change in appetite (increase or decrease)
■ Change in coat (altered colour, different texture, hair loss)
■ Recurrent skin infections
■ Weight gain, weight loss, or inability to lose or gain weight (changes may be subtle, developing over a long time)
■ Lethargy and tiredness (may not be related to aging)

Diabetes mellitus

Insulin is a hormone produced by the pancreas to control the level of glucose in the blood. A deficiency in insulin results in diabetes mellitus, or "sugar diabetes".

Common signs of diabetes mellitus are ravenous hunger, weight loss, abnormal thirst, and frequent passing of large volumes of urine. Occasionally, the first indication may be loss of vision due to a cataract (clouding of the lens of the eye). Sometimes, the disorder may not be diagnosed until a dog becomes unwell from complications arising from diabetes mellitus and has to undergo investigations.

Diabetes mellitus is treated with injections of insulin, together with regular feeding and exercise. Many owners are initially worried about injecting their dogs, but this soon becomes part of the daily routine.

A bitch may develop diabetes mellitus after being in season. Neutering may be the cure, provided there are enough insulin-producing cells remaining in the pancreas. Obesity is another risk factor for developing diabetes mellitus. The disorder seems to be more common

▲ **Tired all the time**
If your dog seems to be sleeping more than usual and is generally less active, he may not be slowing up with age but have a health problem such as an underactive thyroid.

► **Excessive thirst**
An increased thirst is a common sign of a hormonal disorder such as diabetes mellitus or Cushing's syndrome.

in certain breeds, such as the miniature and toy poodles, some terriers, and the Samoyed.

Hypothyroidism

In this condition, there is underproduction of the hormones produced by the thyroid gland in the neck. Hypothyroidism tends to develop in middle-aged dogs, but may appear at a younger age in breeds predisposed to the disorder, such as the Irish Setter, Old English Sheepdog, Dobermann, and Boxer. Hypothyroidism can have diverse effects. Typical signs of an underactive thyroid gland include weight gain that is difficult to reverse and lethargy. There may be changes in coat colour, thinning of the coat leading to fur loss, and skin infections. Hypothyroidism is diagnosed from blood tests and treated with thyroid hormone replacement, given by tablet.

Cushing's syndrome

Mostly seen in middle-aged or older dogs, Cushing's syndrome is the result of abnormally high blood levels of cortisol – a hormone produced by the adrenal glands. Signs are increased appetite and thirst, increased urination, hair loss, development of a pot-belly, and blackheads on the skin. There may be slow healing of wounds, breathlessness, and lethargy. Diagnosis is based on blood and urine tests, radiography, and ultrasound. Treatment is usually with drugs; if an adrenal tumour is the cause of the high cortisol levels, surgery may be possible.

Addison's disease

In Addison's disease the adrenal glands do not produce enough of the hormones cortisol and aldosterone. The deficiency interferes with the

Living with Addison's disease
A dog with Addison's disease can lead a normal life once he is on treatment. In stressful situations, such as going into kennels, he may require additional drugs to help him cope.

balance of sodium and potassium in the blood, and affects the ability to cope with stress. The disease typically affects young or middle-aged female dogs and is sometimes caused by sudden withdrawal of corticosteroid drugs.

Signs of Addison's disease can be vague: vomiting, diarrhoea, loss of appetite, weight loss, and increased thirst. Occasionally, these signs become much more severe, and the dog collapses in a so-called "Addisonian crisis". Diagnosis is by blood and urine tests; treatment involves hormone replacement with tablets, and monitoring with regular blood screening.

Dwarfism

The hormone that regulates growth is produced by the pituitary gland, situated just beneath the brain. In the congenital disorder known as dwarfism, there is underproduction of this growth hormone and normal development is affected. In a puppy with dwarfism, the head, body, and limbs may all be in proportion but undersized; or just one area of the body, such as the legs, may be abnormal. The adult coat does not grow, so alopecia develops as the puppy coat is lost and not replaced. The dog has a shrill bark, and may show no signs of sexual maturity.

Dwarfism can be treated with injections of growth hormone together with supplementation of thyroid hormone. Affected dogs have a shortened lifespan.

Immune system disorders

The normal role of the immune system is to fight disease and protect the body from harm. When it goes wrong, the system may not provide enough protection, or it may become overactive and itself cause a disorder.

Signs of a problem

- Itchy skin (allergy)
- Swelling of lymph nodes (lymphoma)
- Lethargy
- High temperature
- Scales and crusting on nose (discoid lupus erythematosus)
- Spontaneous bleeding (thrombocytopaenia)

Allergies

An allergy is an over-reaction of the immune system to a substance usually considered harmless (an allergen). Flea allergic dermatitis is a common skin disorder in dogs (p.96) resulting from an allergic response to flea saliva. Some dogs react to environmental allergens, such as pollen, that are inhaled or come into contact with the skin. Hypersensitivity to certain foods can also cause a reaction.

Typically, signs of an allergy – most commonly, itchy skin – first appear in the young dog. Strict flea control is vital, and a food trial to identify any food hypersensitivity may make it easier to avoid trigger foods. Treatment is based on shampoos, antibiotics for skin infections, and drugs such as antihistamines or low-dose corticosteroids to reduce the allergic response. Allergens can be identified with skin testing and specific blood tests so that a vaccine can be formulated.

Lymphoma

The lymph nodes are the sentinels of the immune system. These small organs work as filters, trapping bacteria and other harmful substances before they enter the bloodstream. Enlargement of the lymph nodes may be due to injury or infection; more seriously, it can mean a type of cancer known as lymphoma. In dogs, lymphoma may be seen or felt as swellings under either side of the jaw or in front of a shoulder. If the disease has reached an advanced stage, the dog may also be drinking excessively. Diagnosis requires biopsy of an enlarged lymph node, blood tests, radiography, and ultrasound scanning. Chemotherapy can be successful in treating lymphoma, especially with an early diagnosis.

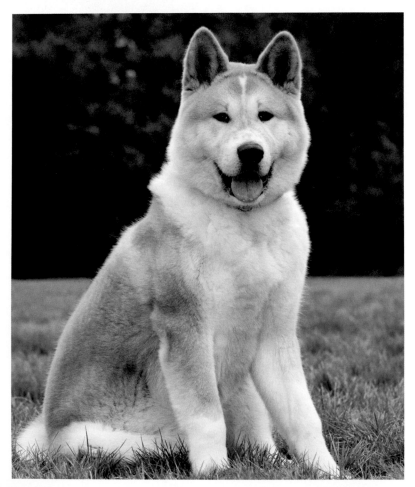

◀ **Allergy prone**
The Japanese Akita is a breed particularly prone to skin allergies. Signs of a possible allergic reaction include excessive licking and scratching all over.

▲ Springer puppy at risk
Immune-mediated haemolytic anaemia occurs in many breeds, including the English Springer Spaniel. The disease may develop gradually or arise suddenly, with pale gums and lethargy.

▲ Destruction of red blood cells
A large blood cell (macrophage) in the immune system destroys the body's own red blood cells, causing immune-mediated haemolytic anaemia.

Immune-mediated disorders

Rarely, the immune system may direct itself against the body's own tissues. This causes a variety of serious diseases, among which is systemic lupus erythematosus (SLE), an inflammatory condition that causes blood-clotting problems, joint pain, skin changes, and fits. Diagnosis may involve blood tests, skin biopsy, and examination of joint fluid. SLE is treated with immunosuppressive drugs. Another form of lupus, cutaneous or discoid lupus erythematosus (DLE) affects the dog's nose, and sometimes other areas of skin, causing scaling, crusting, depigmentation, and ulceration. DLE is diagnosed from skin biopsies. Treatment with creams or ointments may help in mild cases, but immunosuppressive drugs are needed for severe DLE.

Immune-mediated haemolytic anaemia is caused by the destruction of red blood cells.

This disease can be due to another immune disorder such as SLE, infection, or drug treatment. Breeds that are particularly prone include the English Springer Spaniel and American Cocker Spaniel. Signs include lethargy, weakness, pale gums, and fever. Diagnosis is from blood tests, radiography, and ultrasound scanning. This disorder is treated with corticosteroids, specific treatment of an underlying cause if possible, and blood transfusion.

In immune-mediated thrombocytopaenia, there is a low blood platelet count (platelets are the smallest blood cells), which affects normal blood clotting. Signs include pinpoint haemorrhages under the skin, nosebleeds, and bleeding gums. Breeds predisposed to this disorder include the Cocker Spaniel and Poodle. Diagnosis is by blood test and treatment comprises immunosuppressive drug therapy.

External parasites

Even the most well-groomed dog is susceptible to infestation by various skin parasites, some of which are potential carriers of serious diseases. All-year-round prevention is the key to controlling these pests.

Signs of a problem

- Scratching
- Bare patches where hair falls out
- May be scabs and crusting
- May see the actual parasite
- Black debris (flea dirts, which leave tell-tale red streaks when dissolved in water)
- Effects of disease caused by parasite (e.g. in Lyme disease carried by ticks: painful, swollen joints, fever, failure to eat, lethargy, swollen lymph glands; more rarely, neck pain, seizures, kidney failure, heart problems)

Fleas

You need to take all-year-round preventive action against fleas. Running a flea comb through your dog's coat, especially over the rump, may catch fleas, which you can kill by squashing them against the teeth of the comb with a finger. You are more likely to find flea dirts, which show up as black debris. Treatment includes spot-on products (applied at the back of the neck), tablets, and collars. Alternatively, you can spray, wash, or powder your dog. Treat all other pets, including cats and rabbits, at the same time as your dog. Fleas pass most of their life cycle in carpets and furniture, so you may need to use separate products to eradicate them from the home.

Ticks

These unpleasant creatures are a seasonal problem that mostly occurs in spring and autumn. Ticks can attach themselves to your dog and may transmit diseases; for example, some ticks carry the bacterium Borrelia burgdorferi, acquired from mammals such as rodents and deer, which causes Lyme disease in humans and dogs.

Swift removal of a tick reduces the risk of infections. Using tweezers or a tick hook, hold the tick close to the dog's skin but without squeezing its body. Gently twist to remove it. If the head is embedded try to remove that too. Mouthparts left behind can cause a reaction and a lump may develop but treatment is not usually needed and the lump will vanish.

If you live in or are travelling to an area known for ticks, you should take preventive measures such as spot-on treatments and collars.

Mites

The spider-like Sarcoptes mite is commonly passed on to dogs from foxes. It particularly affects the ears, elbows, and hocks, causing sarcoptic mange with intense itchiness, hair loss, and skin sores.

Demodex mites are probably passed from mother to puppies at birth. They affect the skin on the head and around the eyes, and can appear elsewhere, causing fur thinning, bald areas, and a musty smell. These mites may be found in skin scrapings from healthy dogs but they particularly occur at times of stress or illness when a dog's immune system is weakened. Mild demodectic mange resolves without treatment. Severe cases need specific treatment to kill the mites, which is continued until several skin scrapings are clear; antibiotics may also be needed if there is an associated skin infection.

The bright orange, non-parasitic harvest mite is picked up by a dog running in fields in summer. It tends to be found on the skin of the toes, ears, and around the eyes. Harvest mites rub off easily and usually cause no reaction, but they may be linked to a serious disorder called seasonal canine illness.

Lice

A dog who has lice will scratch frequently. The lice can be seen in the coat and on the skin, with nits (eggs) attached to hairs. The entire life cycle of a louse takes place on an individual dog and lasts less than three weeks. Lice are transferred by close contact to other dogs or via grooming tools, but not to people. Your vet will recommend specific treatments.

▶ **Skin parasites**
Lice, fleas, and ticks are common parasites. All have nuisance value, and ticks can transmit disease. Preventive measures and regular checks of your dog's coat keep these pests to a minimum.

Louse   Flea   Tick

Flea hunt
If your dog persistently bites or scratches his coat he is highly likely to be bothered by fleas. These pests cause maddening irritation as they move around and feed on their host's blood.

Internal parasites

Worms that live inside your pet are common and they can be controlled easily with regular treatment. Prevention of internal parasites, rather than having to treat an infestation and its effects, is the ideal.

Signs of a problem

- Always seems hungry but does not gain weight
- General ill-health
- Poor coat
- Bloated belly
- Coughing
- Diarrhoea
- Dragging rear across ground
- Adult worms seen in faeces
- Tapeworm segments (resembling wriggly rice grains) seen around the rear or in faeces.

Roundworm

The adult worms, which look like strands of spaghetti, live in the gut, producing eggs that pass out in the faeces and mature for one to three weeks before being infective to others, including humans. This is why picking up your dog's faeces is so important. A dog can acquire roundworms from the soil or by eating other carriers such as rodents. Puppies can be infected in the womb by roundworm larvae passed on from their mother.

Prevention of roundworms starts with treating the pregnant bitch and continues after birth, both with the puppies and their mother, and at regular intervals throughout life. Ask your vet about which product to use and the worming schedule to follow as your puppy grows up.

Tapeworm

The eggs of the commonest tapeworm species, Dipylidium caninum, are

▼ **Healthy family**
Roundworm prevention for these puppies started before they were born, as their mother was treated during pregnancy. They should be wormed regularly throughout life.

▲ Danger in snails
Lungworm can be picked up if a dog eats an infected snail or slug, either intentionally or accidentally if, for example, there is one on a toy or bowl left outside.

▲ Sources of tapeworms
Dogs are most likely to pick up tapeworms from infected fleas, but other sources of infestation include contaminated raw meat and the carcasses of wildlife such as rodents.

carried by fleas and your dog can become infected by licking fleas off his coat and swallowing them. The adult flat, segmented worm develops within the gut, and sheds egg-containing segments, which you may see as wriggly "rice grains" around your dog's anus or in his faeces. They cause itching, and your dog may "scoot" his bottom along the ground. Treatment comprises tapeworm-specific medication, together with flea control.

Your dog may pick up other tapeworm species from eating offal, raw meat, wild animals, or roadkill. Some tapeworms are a serious health risk to humans.

Lungworm

Also known as French heartworm, this parasite (Angiostrongylus vasorum) is picked up by a dog eating snails and slugs, which can carry the worm larvae. Adult worms develop in the right ventricle (chamber) of the heart and in the pulmonary artery. The females lay eggs containing first-stage larvae, which are carried in the bloodstream to the lungs. Here they hatch out, burrowing into lung tissue

and causing damage. The dog coughs them up and swallows them, passing them out in faeces as a source of further infection to slugs and snails.

Lungworm can be hard to diagnose. Various symptoms may include lethargy, cough, anaemia, nose bleeds, weight loss, poor appetite, vomiting, and diarrhoea. The dog may also display behavioural changes. Diagnostic tests include examining a tracheal wash and faeces, as well as radiography and blood tests.

Your vet will recommend drugs for treatment and prevention of lungworm. Pick up dog faeces promptly (and fox faeces, too, if you find them in the garden). Lungworm cannot be passed directly to other pets or to humans.

Heartworm

This parasite (Dirofilaria immitis) is transmitted by the bite of an infected mosquito. Heartworms live

in the dog's heart, lungs, and surrounding blood vessels, and can cause death if left untreated. Owners in high-risk areas should seek prompt veterinary attention if their dog develops a cough or becomes lethargic during the mosquito season. Diagnosis is by blood test and treatment is risky, requiring the dog to rest for several weeks afterwards. Year-round prevention with heartworm medicines is usually effective.

Preventing worms

Routine worming reduces the likelihood of infestation. Your vet will advise you on the best treatment for your puppy or dog. The ideal programme depends on the perceived risk, which may be high if, for example, you walk your dog in public places, he is a keen scavenger of dead rodents, or he lives with small children. Strict flea control is the key to tapeworm prevention. You must weigh your dog, especially if he is still growing, so that you give the correct dose.

Infectious diseases

Most infectious diseases are caused by bacteria and viruses. Just as in human medicine, bacterial infections in dogs are treated with antibiotics, while many serious viral infections can be avoided with vaccinations.

Signs of a problem

■ Diarrhoea (sometimes bloody), vomiting, and abdominal pains
■ Runny nose, coughing, discharge from eyes (distemper)
■ Hardening of paw pads and nose (distemper)
■ Loss of appetite
■ Weakness, collapse
■ Fever
■ Haemorrhages under the skin, nosebleeds (leptospirosis)

▼ Vulnerable age groups
A dog's age can make a difference to his ability to resist illness or cope with the effects. Very young puppies and very old dogs are most at risk from infectious diseases.

Parvovirus

This dangerous viral infection is typically seen in young dogs that often have not been vaccinated or have not yet completed their course of vaccination. Parvovirus causes acute gastroenteritis, with bloody diarrhoea and vomiting, and can be fatal within just two to three days. The virus, which can survive for months in the environment, is transmitted via infected faeces.

Parvovirus is diagnosed by testing for the virus in faeces as well as by the history and signs of illness. Treatment relies on intensive intravenous fluid therapy, together with a drug to prevent vomiting, and antibiotics to prevent secondary bacterial infection.

Distemper

A highly infectious viral disease, distemper is transmitted through airborne droplets and spreads readily between dogs, especially if they are young and unvaccinated. Initially, the disorder affects the respiratory tract, causing a runny nose, coughing, and discharge from the eyes. Later there is vomiting and diarrhoea, and hardening of the dog's paw pads and nose. The virus is not long-lived in the environment and is easily killed by most household disinfectants.

Diagnosis is from the history and signs. Treatment consists of antibiotics for secondary infection, and intravenous fluids and antiemetics for gastroenteritis.

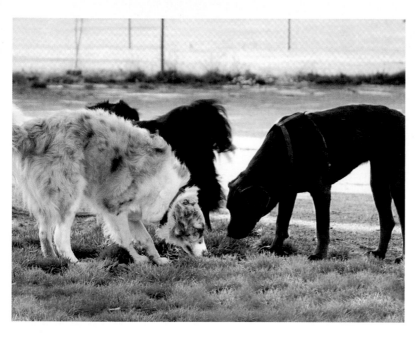

◄ **Passing on infections**
Dogs are sociable and their habit of sniffing each other, and other dogs' urine and faeces, means that infections can spread rapidly among unvaccinated animals.

▼ **Danger on the streets**
Feral dogs roam the streets in many parts of the world, some of them infected with rabies. They should never be handled, however appealing they may seem.

Leptospirosis

Passed on through the urine of an infected animal, leptospirosis is a highly infectious bacterial disease that both dogs and humans can contract. One form, Leptospira icterohaemorrhagiae causes Weil's disease, mainly targeting the liver; it is carried by rats, so dogs can pick up the infection directly from the urine of an infected rat, or when swimming in ditches and ponds. L. canicola is a dog-specific variant that affects the kidneys. Signs can include vomiting, bloody diarrhoea, weakness, and fever.

Leptospirosis is diagnosed from blood and urine tests. Treatment requires long-term antibiotics and intravenous fluids, and the dog must be nursed in isolation.

Rabies

The rabies virus, which can also infect humans, is transmitted in saliva through the bite of an infected animal, although being bitten does not inevitably lead to development of the disease. Rabies can cause seizures, painful throat spasms, and paralysis, and once the disease has developed it is nearly always fatal. Diagnosis is based on the history and signs of illness (and can be confirmed by a post-mortem examination of the brain). Fortunately, the vaccines now available for both humans and dogs are very effective.

Campylobacter and salmonella

These are both bacterial diseases characterized by gastroenteritis, and can be passed either way between humans and dogs. The initial infection is acquired from contaminated food or water.

Diagnosis of campylobacter and salmonella is from testing fresh faecal samples. These diseases are treated with intravenous fluid therapy, and specific antibiotics. Preventive measures against infection include avoiding raw and undercooked meat and covering all food against flies.

Vaccination

Protecting your dog against infection is one of the best things you can do for him. Vaccination has greatly reduced the incidence of major canine diseases such as parvovirus and distemper and prevents other infections, including rabies and leptospirosis. During pregnancy, a bitch (provided her vaccinations are up to date) passes immunity on to her puppies. This protection lasts for a few weeks after birth, then the puppies should be vaccinated. Your vet will recommend when boosters should be given. Some vaccines can give up to three years protection against certain diseases, following a booster 12 months after the initial course.

> **"Viral diseases spread readily between dogs, especially the young and unvaccinated."**

Alternative therapies

Many veterinary surgeons use alternative therapies, often also referred to as complementary therapies, alongside conventional medicine. Ask your vet if such treatments could be of benefit to your dog.

Manipulative therapy

A few types of complementary therapy can be applied to animals by practitioners who are not registered veterinary surgeons. These are forms of manipulation such as osteopathy, physiotherapy, and chiropractic, which may help a back problem, for example. Your dog must, however, be referred to a practitioner by a vet who has examined him, reached a diagnosis, and decided that he may benefit from manipulative treatment of this kind.

Acupuncture

Only a registered veterinary surgeon who has undergone specific training may perform acupuncture on an animal. In this therapy, fine, solid needles are inserted into specific areas of the body referred to as acupuncture points, blocking pain signals, and trigger points. Acupuncture is also believed to stimulate the release of endorphins, body chemicals that act as natural painkillers and increase feelings of well-being.

Acupuncture is particularly useful for dogs with chronic pain associated with arthritis or injuries, for example; it may also help with other problems, although this role is less recognized. The therapy is usually tolerated very well by dogs, especially if they are bribed with food while treatment is taking place. The needles will be left in place for up to 30 minutes, and may be moved to provide additional stimulation. The dog can move around with the needles in place, or lie down. Some

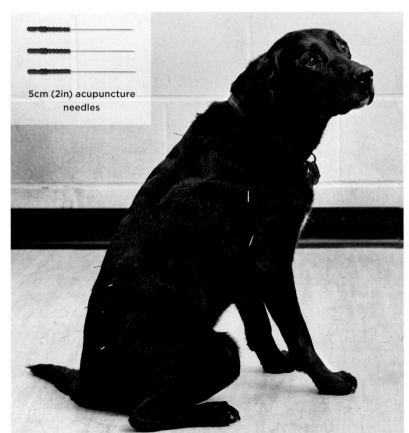

5cm (2in) acupuncture needles

◄ **Acupuncture**
The needles used in acupuncture are sterile and disposable, a fresh set being used for each dog. How many are used, where they are inserted, how long they are left in place, and how much they are moved, determine the treatment "dose".

▼ **Physiotherapy**
Your vet may refer your dog for physiotherapy to help him recover after surgery or an injury. Elderly dogs with arthritic joints can also benefit from this treatment.

dogs become very sleepy during the acupuncture session and may sleep for a while afterwards.

For a day or so after having acupuncture, it is not unusual for symptoms to become worse, rather than improving. If the deterioration persists, your dog's therapist will adjust the treatment at the next session. There are some dogs who do not respond to acupuncture at all, just as there are humans for whom the therapy has no benefit.

Acupuncture sessions are usually weekly at first, with your dog's progress and response being monitored. According to what suits the individual dog, treatments will probably then be spaced further apart.

Hydrotherapy

Swimming is a non-weight-bearing form of exercise that is very beneficial for joint problems and can also help with weight-loss, stamina, and building up muscle after surgery, for example. Hydrotherapy adds to these

benefits by providing controlled conditions for water-based exercises. Most dogs enjoy using the facilities at a hydrotherapy centre, which can vary from a simple pool to an aquatic tread mill. The pool water will be heated to a comfortably warm temperature, and its quality is monitored regularly. There will be facilities for drying your

dog off afterwards to prevent him from becoming cold and stiffening up.

Your vet will refer your dog for hydrotherapy if it looks likely that treatment will be of benefit. Ideally, anyone offering hydrotherapy for dogs should be qualified and registered with an appropriate professional body.

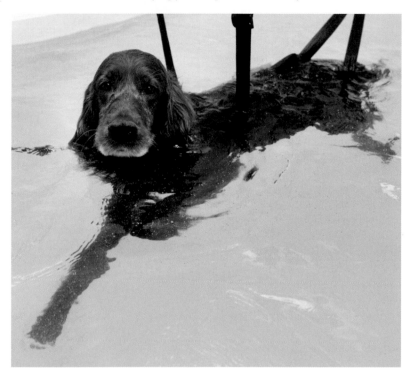

► **Hydrotherapy**
If your dog likes swimming, you should have no difficulty with him accepting hydrotherapy, which offers carefully planned, supervised exercises in warm water.

Herbal and homeopathic treatments

Only a registered veterinary surgeon may treat a dog with herbal and homeopathic therapies. Herbal medicine, which is based on natural substances, may sound innocuous but remedies can include very powerful active agents that can be dangerous in certain circumstances, for example when taken in conjunction with other drugs. Many common health problems in dogs, ranging from allergies to arthritis, skin disorders, and anxiety, may respond to herbal remedies. If you use herbal medicines

for your dog, follow your vet's instructions carefully. Homeopathy treats the underlying disease process, not the outward signs, and takes a holistic approach that includes character and lifestyle. This therapy is based on the theory of using "like to cure like", whereby a substance that causes certain symptoms in a healthy body can, when given in minute doses, cure illnesses that cause the same signs.

▲ **Homeopathic remedies**
Many homeopathic medicines are available in liquid form and can be dropped directly onto the dog's tongue or added to water.

Nursing a sick dog

There may come a time when your dog needs nursing because he is ill or recovering from surgery and cannot manage things he usually does on his own. Follow your vet's instructions and ask for advice if in doubt.

Home care after surgery

Dogs are rarely kept in overnight after neutering or other routine operations, but the vet will give you advice on any specific health care that is needed. Your dog may be discharged with medication such as pain relief, but if he seems uncomfortable then contact the vet. Exercise immediately after surgery should be restricted unless you are advised otherwise.

Contrary to popular belief, a dog does more harm than good if he licks at an undressed wound, which will become sore and infected. Most dogs accept wearing an Elizabethan collar or similar device, and anti-lick strips can also deter an inquisitive tongue and stop dogs from removing dressings on paws and legs.

▶ **Elizabethan collar**
Your dog may not be able to reach his food and water bowls whilst wearing an Elizabethan collar so you will need to remove it periodically.

▲▶ **Adding medicine to food**
This is an easy way to give your dog medication, provided he eats the food. Check the directions first: some medications need to be taken on an empty stomach, or must not be crushed.

Keep dressings clean and dry by covering with a boot or plastic bag when you take your dog outside to do his business. If he worries at a dressing excessively, or it becomes smelly or soiled, then seek your vet's advice as soon as possible.

Giving medication

Prescribed medication should be given to your dog as directed by your vet, and only by an adult. Make sure other pets do not take a drug accidentally, especially if it is given in food. If your dog is prescribed an antibiotic, it is important that he completes the full course. A liquid medication may need to be shaken to ensure thorough mixing before the dose is given. If you are injecting your dog with, for example, insulin, then strictly follow your vet's instructions about storage and administration.

> "A post-operative dog needs rest in a warm, quiet, undisturbed place."

Giving medication directly by mouth is ideal, as you will be sure that your dog has swallowed it. Speak to your vet if this is difficult, as some medications can be hidden in food or a treat (although not if they must be taken on an empty stomach). Unless the tablet is palatable, avoid crushing and mixing it with food, as your dog may then refuse to eat and will not receive the medication. Some tablets must only be given whole.

If your dog develops symptoms such as an upset stomach (vomiting or diarrhoea) while on medication, then discontinue the treatment until you have spoken to a vet.

◄ **Liquid medicine**
If the prescribed medication is a suspension, shake the bottle to ensure thorough mixing. Remove the dose and give to your dog directly into his mouth or with food.

▼ **Sleeping it off**
Following surgery your dog will probably spend more time asleep than usual. Find him a cosy place, where he can let his body recover.

Food and water

Ensure your dog can reach his food and water bowls comfortably, perhaps raising them off the ground so that he has no need to reach down. You may be given a prescription diet to help your dog's recovery but if he will not eat it ask your vet about alternative suitable foods. A similar problem may occur with your dog refusing to drink recommended rehydration fluids. In this case, encourage him to drink cooled, boiled water, which is better than taking no fluids at all.

Rest and exercise

A post-operative dog needs to rest in a quiet place at a warm, not hot, temperature with comfortable bedding. He may prefer to sleep away from the family, or he may seek company. Short walks just pottering around the garden are also important to keep the joints, bladder, and bowel functioning.

Caring for an elderly dog

It is hard to accept that a beloved dog is showing the effects of ageing, but you can help him to go on enjoying life, albeit at a slower pace. A little extra care can make a big difference to your senior dog's wellbeing.

Feeling comfortable

Older dogs tend to be more affected than younger ones by extremes of temperature. Small dogs and naturally lean, thin-coated breeds like greyhounds and whippets may feel the cold more as they age and will benefit from wearing a coat in chilly weather. Remember to remove the coat when your dog is in warmer surroundings or else he will overheat, and never leave a dog in a wet coat. If the weather is particularly warm, a desk fan is a great comfort to a hot dog.

Diet and exercise

Your senior dog will naturally sleep more and be less active, but it is important not to let him become

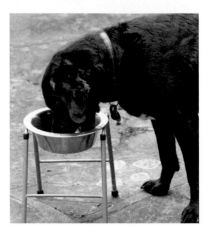

▲ Raised food bowl
Simply raising your dog's feeding bowl may restore his enjoyment of eating. You can buy a stand or improvise with blocks or a step.

▼ Wrapping up
Keep your senior dog warm in a coat chosen from the wide range available, or tailor-make one from a blanket.

overweight. Combat a spreading waistline with regular exercise and senior foods specially formulated to be less energy-dense. Frequent short walks are more suitable than one daily marathon if your dog is struggling to keep up. Very elderly dogs can just potter in the garden and rest whenever they want.

Your dog's mobility may start to be restricted by arthritis. He may find it difficult to jump into the car or to negotiate steps. Lift him into the car if he is not too heavy, or teach him to use a ramp instead. Ramps can also be placed over steps to convert them into a gentle incline. If your dog's neck is stiff, raising his food and water bowls on special stands (or improvising with bricks) should help

► **Taking it easy**
Take your older dog for frequent short walks over a familiar route, on a lead if he needs the security. Be prepared to amble at his pace.

him to eat and drink comfortably. If an arthritic dog finds it hard to curl round to fit in his basket, spread a bigger area of firm and supportive bedding directly on the floor.

An elderly dog needs grooming more often when he cannot reach round to clean himself effectively. Keep the grooming sessions short to avoid tiring him.

Being stiff is painful. Ask your vet about joint supplements and medications that might help your dog to move more easily.

Senior clinic

Your veterinary practice may offer a senior clinic where the focus is on easing your dog through his later years. You will be given advice on such issues as ideal body weight, nutritional supplements, changes in behaviour and eating habits, and

exercise. A clinic can help you to detect problems early and enable treatment to be started as soon as possible. For example, a simple test to assess how much your dog is drinking may provide the impetus for further investigation.

Senility and confusion

Many older dogs are in good physical health but showing signs of senility and confusion. Maintaining a daily routine in familiar surroundings helps them to feel secure. Your vet can tell you about drugs that may help.

◄ **Weight watching**
Monitoring your older dog's weight is a simple aid to good health. Unintentional weight loss may be an early sign of a problem.

Euthanasia

There may come a time when, after careful thought and consideration, you decide to have an old dog euthanased if his quality of life is poor. This can be performed only by a veterinary surgeon, either at your home or in the veterinary practice. A drug is given by intravenous injection into a front leg vein and the vet may give your dog a sedative first. There may be involuntary movements and the bladder or bowels may empty, but many dogs pass away peacefully.
It is a good idea to decide in advance how you want your dog's body handled afterwards, rather than facing the issue on what will be a distressing day.

5

Canine emergencies

Basic first aid

Dogs are inquisitive by nature and do not understand danger the way we do. It is impossible to prevent accidents from happening, so be prepared to provide emergency care if your dog, or someone else's, is injured.

Helping an injured dog

An injured dog usually needs to be examined by a veterinary surgeon. If you know the basic rules of first aid, you will be able to provide help until the vet arrives, or the dog can be transported to a surgery.

When attending to an injured dog, you may need to muzzle him; if he is in pain and frightened he may snap. Move him only if absolutely necessary or if you are sure moving him will not cause further injuries. In the case of bleeding, attempt to stem the flow of blood from any major wounds with direct pressure, carefully raising the injured area above the level of the heart if possible (pp.136–7).

Bear in mind that there are parts of the world where dogs may have rabies. If you are in such an area and see a dog requiring help, you should keep at a safe distance and call an animal control organization.

At home, it is useful to keep your vet's telephone number somewhere handy: by the telephone, stored on your mobile phone, or behind a fridge magnet. Make sure you know what arrangements are in place for obtaining veterinary attention if it is needed outside normal surgery hours.

Recovery position

If an injured dog is unconscious, put him in the recovery position. To do this, remove the dog's collar and place him on his right side, with his head and neck in line with his body. Gently pull his tongue forwards to hang out of the side of his mouth. Feel for a heartbeat and a pulse on the inside of the thigh. Look for chest movements and feel for breath from the nostrils. If the dog is not breathing or his heart has stopped, start resuscitation.

Resuscitation

Hopefully, if you find yourself in a situation where a dog needs to be resuscitated, there will be someone to help you. It is important to stay calm, although this can be difficult.

A dog's heart may stop beating or his respiration fail following an accident involving electrocution or drowning, for example, or after a fit. His best chance of recovery is at a veterinary practice but resuscitation needs to be started immediately once the need has been identified. Ring a vet for advice or,

First aid kit

Accidents can happen at any time, so always keep a few basic first aid necessities to hand. Compact kits equipped with a range of items for dealing with minor emergencies are readily available. These are particularly useful for taking in the car or carrying in a backpack on long walks.

First aid box

Saline wash

Cotton wool

Thermometer

Disposable gloves

Adhesive bandage

Bandage

Scissors

▲ In safe hands
The best place for an injured dog is obviously a veterinary surgery. But if you cannot take him there straight away, you may be able to help him by using simple first aid.

"If you know the basic rules of first aid, you will be able to provide help until the vet arrives."

ideally, ask someone else to make the call while you place the dog in the recovery position. Before attempting resuscitation, check the airway for any obstruction at the back of the mouth.

If the dog is not breathing, start artificial respiration. Place your hands one over the other on the chest wall, just behind the shoulders. Apply a sharp downward movement every 3–5 seconds, allowing the chest wall to spring back in between each thrust, until voluntary breath movements occur.

Check for the dog's circulation by feeling for a pulse (on the inside of the thigh) and a heartbeat (on the side of the chest just behind

▲ Resuscitation
If a dog's heart has stopped beating, his chances of recovery depend on resuscitation being started within a few minutes. Cardiac massage to keep the circulation going is a simple technique that can be life-saving.

the elbow). If the heart has stopped, begin cardiac massage. The massage technique varies according to the size of the dog.
■ Small dog – place the fingers and thumb of one hand around the dog's chest just behind the elbow and

squeeze them together twice per second while your other hand is supporting the spine.
■ Medium-sized dog – place the heel of one hand on the dog's chest just behind the elbow; place your other hand on top and press down on the chest approximately 80-100 times per minute.
■ Large or overweight dog – instead of placing him in the recovery position, lay the dog on his back with his head slightly lower than his body if possible. Place one hand on his chest over the lower end of the breastbone with your other hand on top and apply compressions directed towards the dog's head approximately 80-100 times per minute.

In every, check for a pulse after 15 seconds of applying compressions. If the heartbeat is still absent, continue with cardiac massage until you feel a pulse. If someone else is with you, they can give artificial respiration at the same time.

Deciding how long to continue resuscitation is difficult. If you can act quickly enough, you may keep the dog's brain adequately supplied with oxygen. But unless resuscitation starts within 3–4 minutes of the heart stopping, there is an increased likelihood of irreversible brain damage. In an ideal situation, a vet would pass a tube into the main airway to continue artificial respiration, and would give the dog drugs to help restore heart function.

Wounds and burns

Never leave a wound to heal itself – even the smallest injury can become infected, especially when a dog licks it. If your dog has a severe wound or burns from any source, seek veterinary help as soon as possible.

Minor wounds

If a wound has been caused by another dog or pet then it should be seen by a vet as soon as possible, as it is likely to become infected. However, a small clean wound can be treated at home. Gently flush the wound with saline solution (ready-prepared, or a teaspoon of salt dissolved in a half litre of warm water) to remove any dirt or debris. Carefully cut away hair from around the wound using blunt-ended scissors.

Apply a dressing or bandage, if possible, to prevent your dog from licking at the wound: you may think licking will help the wound to heal, but it is more likely to cause infection. Use appropriate materials if you have them to hand, or improvise with socks or tights to cover a wound on a limb, or a T-shirt for wounds on the chest or abdomen. Use adhesive tape rather than safety pins to hold a bandage in place. Take care not to apply the bandage too tightly, keep it dry, and change it regularly to check on the wound.

Always seek advice if you notice an offensive smell or if a discharge seeps through the bandage.

More serious wounds

A deep or extensive wound needs urgent veterinary attention. Call the vet practice to inform them of the

◄ Worrying at a wound
A bandage protects a wound, especially from a dog's tongue, but if your dog will not leave the bandage alone, he should wear an Elizabethan collar to prevent him causing further damage.

situation and to tell them when you are likely to arrive. Apply a temporary bandage as best you can to stem bleeding.

If the wound is on a limb, raise it above the level of the heart if possible, apply direct pressure via swabs or other padding, and bandage the pad in place. A tourniquet is not advised. Take great care if a foreign body is stuck in the wound: avoid pushing it in more deeply and do not attempt to remove it yourself.

For a wound on the chest, apply swabs soaked with warm saline solution or cooled boiled water and hold them in place with bandaging or a T-shirt.

A wound on the ear flap will spray blood whenever your dog shakes his head. Cover the wound with a swab and bandage the ear flap to his head (p.100).

After-care will depend on the nature of the wound. Bandages will need to be changed every 2–5 days as advised by your vet. All bandages must be kept dry, so cover them with a waterproof outer layer when your dog goes outside to relieve himself.

Burns

Painful and sometimes severe damage to the skin can be caused by contact with heat, electricity, or chemicals.

Burns from fire or a hot object such as an iron, or scalding with hot liquid are treated in the same way. Remove your dog from the source of the injury without endangering yourself, then contact your vet for advice; a burn or scald can be very serious, with hidden

---

"A wound caused by another dog or pet should be seen by a vet as it is likely to become infected."

---

damage to deep tissues. Flood the area with cold water for at least ten minutes then cover with a moist sterile dressing or cling film to prevent contamination and stop your dog from interfering with the burn. Keep him warm and as still as possible whilst taking him to the vet. He will be given pain relief, and treatment for shock if the area affected is extensive.

Electrical burns in the mouth through biting a power cable are common. Turn off the power at source before handling your dog. Urgent veterinary attention will be needed for pain relief and also because an electric shock can cause dangerous complications.

If your dog has been burned by chemicals, take care not to contaminate yourself. Identify and note down the substances involved and contact your vet. If appropriate, the vet may advise you to flush the area with water, but you must be careful to avoid spreading the chemicals further.

How to bandage a paw

Apply a sterile dressing. Run a soft conforming bandage down the front of the leg, over the paw, up behind, then back to the paw and up the front again.

Wind the bandage around the leg down to the paw and then back up the leg. Repeat the earlier steps with an elasticated gauze bandage.

Repeat with a final cohesive layer, running it up on to the fur to secure it. Zinc oxide tape can also be used to secure the top of the dressing.

Fitting

Convulsions, or fits, are due to abnormal electrical activity in the brain. In a young dog, the cause is likely to be epilepsy; the reasons for the onset of fitting in an older dog vary but could include a brain tumour.

Signs of fitting

Seeing a dog have a convulsion or fit is very alarming. All you can do is clear the area around your dog so that he cannot harm himself, and contact the vet for advice. Make a note of when the fit occurred and any details that could be relevant, such as whether the television was on at the time, and whether your dog had eaten recently or just come back from a walk. If you have an un-neutered bitch, note if it is around the time of her season.

Fitting classically occurs when a dog is dozing. You may have noticed your dog acting strangely beforehand, but a fit can also be totally unexpected. Signs of fitting may be trembling and twitching, or your dog may lie on his side, with his legs paddling as if he was running. (Dogs commonly do this when they are "dreaming", but they will respond when called or touched.) Your dog may also salivate and chomp his jaws, empty his bowels, and urinate. A fit lasts from only seconds to a few minutes. Your dog may be aggressive during a fit or in recovery. He may rapidly return to normal, but he could be distant and disorientated for a few hours.

A dog may have more than one fit within a few hours or days of each other. More worryingly, he may have a run of fits, where he is not fully conscious between each episode. This is called status epilepticus and is a real emergency needing veterinary attention.

Treating fits

After a fit, the vet will give your dog a thorough examination, including a full neurological investigation, and will probably advise that blood tests be carried out. Normal results often lead to a diagnosis of idiopathic epilepsy (that is, of no known cause) but cannot rule out brain tumour, for which an MRI scan would be needed.

For an intact bitch who is having fits, neutering will be advised by the vet. There are various drug options for treating epilepsy, although the vet may not start treatment after just one fit. Side effects can include drowsiness and weight gain. Regular monitoring is needed to ensure that the drug is at the correct level in the blood to control fitting without causing adverse effects. Over time, the dosage may have to be increased or other drugs added. To treat status epilepticus, the dog is kept under a general anaesthetic until the vet allows recovery of consciousness in the hope that fitting will not resume.

> "After a fit your dog may rapidly return to normal, but he could be distant and disorientated for a few hours."

◄ **TV trigger**
The flickering light of a television screen is sometimes found to be the cause of a dog having a fit, but more commonly the triggers of fitting are not so obvious.

Road traffic accidents

Take every precaution to protect your dog from traffic accidents and prevent him from endangering other road users. Always keep him on a lead when walking on or near a road, however well trained he may be.

Emergency aid

If a dog is injured in a road traffic accident, ring a veterinary surgeon for advice. Also contact the police if the accident happened on a public highway. Legally, the driver of the vehicle that hit the dog must stop and give his or her details to the person in charge of the dog. If the dog is on its own then the driver must report the incident to the police within 24 hours.

The dog may have open wounds, internal injuries, fractures, or a combination of injuries. Move him only if you feel it will not cause further injury, or if there is a danger of the dog being hit by another vehicle. Above all, take care not to endanger yourself. Using a blanket as a stretcher between two people is ideal. Carefully manoeuvre the dog onto it whilst bearing in mind that a dog in pain

may snap without warning and without meaning to do so. If you are on your own, and the casualty is not a big dog, then it may be a matter of having to scoop him up in your arms to remove him out of the path of traffic.

If you can transport the injured dog to a vet practice yourself, telephone ahead to advise that you are on your way. Otherwise, keep the casualty warm whilst waiting

> "Move a dog only if it will not cause further injury. Take care not to endanger yourself."

▼ Waiting for help
An injured dog may be unconscious or conscious and probably shocked and in pain. Keep him warm until help comes. Make sure that you do not put yourself at risk to tend to him.

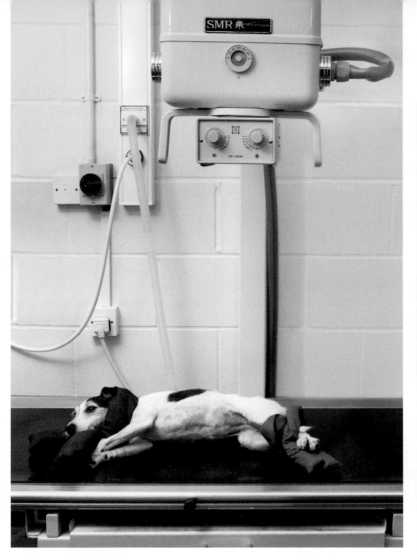

Minimizing the risks

■ Keep your dog on a short lead when walking along the side of any road or lane.
■ Keep garden gates closed and boundaries secure so your dog cannot escape.
■ Make sure your dog is obedient and responds immediately to your commands of stay and sit.

for help to arrive. A foil survival blanket would be ideal if available but improvising with anything such as a warm coat or jumper will still improve the dog's chances of survival. If there is heavy bleeding, apply pressure with a pad.

If the injured dog is not with his owner, look for identification. He should have a disc on his collar engraved with contact details for his owner. Failing that, his breed, colour, sex, and approximate age will help with identification later. If a microchip is found when he is scanned, then contacting the owner should be straightforward,

provided the owner has kept his registration information up to date.

Treatment

Once at the veterinary practice, the priorities will be to provide pain relief, treat the dog for shock with intravenous fluids, and establish the extent of the injuries. Knowledge of pre-existing conditions and medications will be invaluable but only likely if the dog has been identified and there is full access to his medical history.

Before giving treatment, the vet will do blood tests to gather information about the dog's general

health and to look for signs of internal injuries. Radiography of the chest and abdomen, coupled with ultrasound scanning, will help to identify internal bleeding and organ damage. Fractures may be suspected from a physical examination of the dog, and can be confirmed with radiography of the appropriate areas.

Except in the case of life-threatening problems that call for immediate surgery, such as a major haemorrhage, an operation requiring general anaesthetic will be postponed until the dog's condition is stable.

Choking and poisoning

It is in a dog's nature to chew or eat anything that looks promising, but it is a habit that can get him into serious trouble. If your dog chokes on something or swallows a poisonous substance, you need to act quickly.

Choking

A dog can choke on all manner of objects, including bones, rawhide chews, wood, or children's toys. He may paw frantically at his mouth if the object is wedged between his teeth or across the roof of his mouth, and he may have difficulty breathing if the object is obstructing his airway. He may also drool profusely.

Only attempt to retrieve the object from your dog's mouth if you will not be bitten or there is no risk of pushing it further into the throat. Putting something across your dog's jaw to prevent him from closing his mouth is a good idea if it does not make it harder to retrieve the object. Ideally, use something rubbery or a pad of material to avoid damaging his teeth; never use a muzzle.

If you cannot remove the object, or are concerned that your dog's mouth has been damaged, then reassure him and take him straight to a vet. Telephone first to tell them there is an emergency.

If you see your dog swallow something he should not, such as a small piece of jewellery, a button, or a stone, contact your vet for advice. Very small objects may pass through your dog without causing a problem. A larger item may cause a blockage and need to be removed, preferably from the stomach through an endoscope before it has entered the intestines.

Poisoning

The commonest way for a dog to be poisoned is by scavenging something not intended for him. If you are worried that your dog may have eaten forbidden foods or substances, or he has persistent

▼ **Dangerous bones**
A bone can pose a choking hazard if it is small enough to become wedged across the roof of the mouth or between the teeth, or if shards are swallowed and become stuck in the gullet.

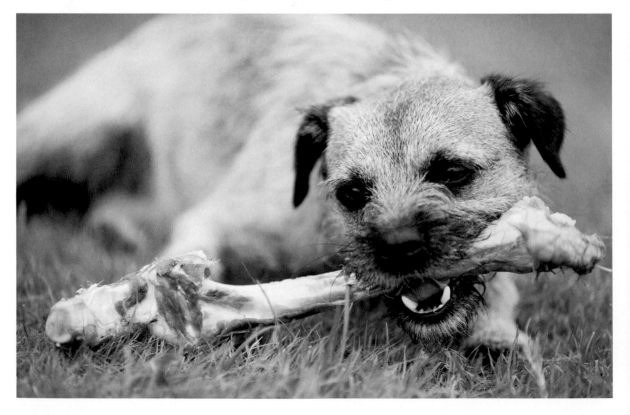

► Algae risk

Some species of blue-green algae found in both fresh and salt water can cause fatal poisoning. If your dog loves a dip, try to find out if there is any record of contaminated water in your area.

▼ Raiding the bin

A dog's dietary indiscretions include raiding the rubbish bin. Use containers such as pedal operated or mechanical push opening bins, which will not yield to a dog's questing nose.

vomiting or diarrhoea, contact your veterinary practice straight away for advice, because taking early action can be life-saving. Keep any packaging to show the vet.

The home is potentially a very dangerous place (pp.18–19). It is extraordinary just what a dog will eat, given the chance. Take preventive action by always storing anything remotely edible out of reach. This includes all medication, both veterinary and human; anti-freeze (ethylene glycol) which has a sweet taste but will cause kidney failure if drunk by a dog; weedkillers and slug bait, which are easily picked up in the garden; and household cleaners (even if you keep them in an inaccessible

cupboard, remember that your dog may drink from a lavatory which has a chemical released into the water whenever it is flushed).

Among foodstuffs, chocolate is highly appealing to a dog but is toxic if it has a high cocoa solid content. Onions and their relations, including leeks, garlic, and spring onions, are also poisonous to dogs.

Generally, the smaller the dog, the smaller the amount of toxin needed to have an effect. However, this is not the case with grapes both fresh and dried (raisins, sultanas, and currants), which are recognized as potential poisons.

A small dog may eat a bunch of grapes and have no problems, whilst a large

dog may eat only a few and be very ill. The dried grapes, ingredients in many foodstuffs such as cakes, are by far the most toxic and eating them can lead to serious problems such as kidney failure and pancreatitis.

Rat poison

Bait to control rodents should be used and stored well out of your dog's reach. Commonly available rat poisons interfere with the action of vitamin K, which is essential to the body's normal blood clotting process. This causes internal bleeding, which will not become immediately apparent. If you know or suspect that your dog has eaten rat poison, or a poisoned rodent, contact your vet and take the dog straight to the practice, together with any relevant packaging.

"The home is potentially a very dangerous place. Store anything edible out of reach."

Bites and stings

Dogs are naturally inquisitive, exploring with their noses, so bites and stings from venomous animals or insects tend to be on the head and legs. Identifying the culprit will ensure your dog receives the right treatment.

Snakes

Venomous snakes are encountered in various natural environments worldwide. Their toxicity depends on the species, the amount of venom injected relative to the size of the dog, and the site of the bite.

The effects of a snake bite develop rapidly, within two hours. The puncture wounds from the bite are often visible, with painful swelling developing. A bitten dog may become lethargic and show other signs of poisoning, including overheating, rapid heart rate and panting, pale mucous membranes, excessive salivation, and vomiting. In severe cases, the liver, kidneys, and blood-clotting system may be affected, and the dog may go into shock or a coma.

Do not attempt to suck out the venom or apply a tourniquet. Speed is of the essence, so contact a veterinary practice and go there without delay. If a specific antivenom is to be used in the treatment of your dog, you need to be able to identify what bit him. If you are not certain of the species you could take photographs of the culprit, provided this is possible without endangering yourself.

Bees and wasps

These are a common risk to dogs both indoors and outdoors. If your dog is stung, move him quickly to avoid further stings and to avoid being stung yourself. Carefully check for insects trapped in your dog's coat and look for the site of the sting. Bees leave their stinger behind, so remove it carefully with tweezers if you can do this without squeezing the poison sac. Wasps can sting repeatedly, although they may leave the stinger in the skin. Bathe the area with bicarbonate dissolved in water (for bee stings) or with vinegar (for wasp stings), then apply antihistamine cream. Distract your dog or cover the area to prevent him from licking at it.

If your dog is in pain or his condition deteriorates, take him to the vet. Some dogs develop hives or multiple bumps under the skin. It is an emergency situation if your dog has been stung in the mouth or develops a severe allergic reaction.

Toads

When a toad feels threatened, it releases venom from its skin glands, which may be taken into a dog's mouth if he licks the toad or picks it up. A dog will react to toad venom with excessive salivation and may froth at the mouth and become very anxious. Carefully flush out his mouth with water and seek advice from your vet if you are concerned. The toxicity of toad venom varies between species. Exposure to the venom of the cane toad, Bufo marinus, is a serious situation. Flush out the dog's mouth and take him to a veterinary practice for emergency attention.

Anaphylactic shock

Occasionally, a dog may have an extreme reaction shortly after exposure to something to which he is acutely sensitive – for example, bee venom, especially if he has had multiple stings. This severe allergic reaction, which is known as anaphylactic shock, can be a life-threatening situation. Initial signs of anaphylactic shock include vomiting and excitability, rapidly leading on to breathing difficulties, collapse, coma, and death. Emergency treatment is needed at a veterinary practice if the dog is to survive.

▶ **Creatures to avoid**
A chance encounter with something that bites or stings can be painful and frightening for your dog.

Rattlesnake

Bee

Cane toad

"It is an emergency situation if your dog has been stung and develops an allergic reaction."

Lurking in the undergrowth
Poisonous snakes, stinging insects, and other dangers can remain hidden in long grass until disturbed by an exploring nose. If your dog is bitten or stung, attend to him quickly and keep him calm.

Heat stroke and hypothermia

The effects of either overheating or exposure to cold can be fatal to a dog. Yet, with a little care and forethought, such a disaster is nearly always avoidable. Old or sick dogs and puppies are especially susceptible.

Heat stroke

If a dog overheats he cannot cool down again by sweating as humans do. In such situations as being confined in a car on a hot day or shut in a conservatory at home, especially if there is no drinking water available, your dog can rapidly develop heat stroke. This is a dangerous condition in which the body's temperature-regulating mechanism breaks down. The fashion for "dressing up" dogs in trendy canine clothing has also been responsible for some cases of overheating, particularly where owners have omitted to undress their dogs when indoors.

Heat stroke is a real medical emergency: without urgent veterinary attention, a dog can die from overheating within as little as 20 minutes. Signs include panting, distress, and reddening of the gums, with rapid progression to collapse, coma, and ultimately death. The priority is to remove the dog from the hot place to somewhere cool or take off his unwanted "clothing". If a delay in taking him to a veterinary practice is unavoidable, then you should cover him with wet sheets or towels, which can be kept over him while he is transported. Alternatively, put the dog in a bath of cold water or run a steady stream of water over him from a garden hose. Ice packs or bags of frozen peas can be used, and a fan will also help to cool him down.

Heat stroke is easily avoided simply by not leaving your dog in the car. It really is not enough just to leave the windows open, even if you have parked in the shade. The situation is particularly risky if there are several dogs in the car, or your dog is already hot and panting from recent exercise.

Hypothermia

The reverse of heat stroke is hypothermia, when the body's core temperature falls to dangerously low levels. This is another emergency that is easily avoided. In cold weather, your dog can develop hypothermia if he is kept outside in a draughty kennel, or left in an unheated room or a car. Going into a pond or lake in winter can also lead to hypothermia. Puppies and old dogs are the most vulnerable.

A dog with hypothermia may shiver or move stiffly and appear lethargic. He needs warming up gradually out of the cold and kept covered with a blanket until he can be taken to a vet. A hypothermic dog will be given sterile warm fluids directly into a vein to help restore his core body temperature, together with treatment for shock.

> "Heat stroke is a real medical emergency: without urgent attention a dog can die in 20 minutes."

◄ **Living outside**
A kennel protects your dog from wind and rain, but temperatures inside may soar in summer, and plummet in winter unless you can provide safe heating.

Danger of overheating
Even with the window down, a car quickly becomes an oven, even at only moderately warm temperatures. Left shut in, this dog would be at risk of heat stroke.

6

Breeding

Responsible breeding

Making the decision to breed from your dog should not be taken lightly. Not only is it an expensive and time-consuming process, but it can result in adding to the enormous surplus of dogs without homes.

Consider the reasons

Before you breed from your dog, it is important to think long and hard about your reasons for wanting to have a litter of puppies. Never breed to make money (not least because once you have paid stud fees, equipment costs, and food and vet bills there is little money to be made). It is easy to get carried away with thoughts of cute puppies playing around your home, but the reality is that rearing a litter is extremely hard work. They require daily care and attention as they grow. It may be that your dog has such a lovely temperament or good looks that you feel that it is your duty to create puppies with similar qualities. Unfortunately it is rarely that simple due to the way traits are inherited and there is no guarantee that the next generation will be the same as the last.

If you are considering breeding because you want another dog yourself, spare a thought for the hundreds of thousands of dogs in rescue homes and shelters. There are many benefits from adopting an older dog (pp.12–3). Often they may already be house-trained and socialized and any personality traits or problem behaviours are already evident. This makes it easier to pick a dog that suits your temperament and lifestyle.

If you have your heart set on a puppy it is best to find a reputable

> "Before you breed from your dog, think long and hard – never breed to make money."

Non-pedigree pregnancies

If you do not intend to breed from your bitch, it is advisable to have her neutered. However, occasionally accidents happen and unplanned matings occur. Speak to your vet immediately to discuss your options as it may be that stopping the pregnancy is advisable for the health of your bitch. It could also be that the other dog is unknown to you or he has no pedigree, in which case you should speak to your vet about the best ways to re-home the puppies when they are born.

◄ **Handling new lives**
Puppies are an adorable addition to any household but they require a huge investment of time and effort. The first few weeks will determine a puppy's character for life so you need to give them full-time care and attention.

▲ Pedigree pair
When choosing the perfect breeding partner, make sure you know the ancestry of both dogs; it helps to determine how closely related they are to prevent inbreeding.

▶ Mating call
In season bitches release a powerful scent to advertise their desire to mate. If your bitch is in season and not neutered yet, she may become pregnant if allowed to wander.

professional breeder who can also give you the reassurance of their years of experience.

If you are still set on having pups from your current dog, first ask yourself the following questions:
■ Can you find homes for all the puppies?
■ Do you have the knowledge to advise these potential owners, some of whom may never have owned a dog before?
■ Do you have the flexibility to spend weeks at home looking after the puppies once they are born?
■ Do you have adequate space, not just for the litter to be born but for a litter of 6-week-old puppies?

If you have considered everything and are still certain breeding from your dog

is the right decision, do lots of research and plan everything carefully.

The perfect partner

Deciding which dog to mate with yours is a difficult decision. Always consult with a breed specialist to discuss possible inherited diseases and disorders such as hip dysplasia, blindness, and deafness (pp.92–3). You may also want to carry out screening tests that will help detect any potential conditions and eliminate the likelihood of these diseases occurring. Analyse where your dog has weaknesses and choose a mate that can improve upon those areas. Research the pedigree of both dogs to spot potential problems. Remember even an ideal screening result will not

guarantee that your puppy won't develop a chronic disorder.

When you have chosen your stud dog, always meet him to make sure his temperament is exemplary. Work out when your bitch comes into season – it may vary from breed to breed – and contact the stud dog owner to arrange when and where the dogs will meet. Monitor the mating process but ideally do not interfere too closely. Time will tell if your bitch is pregnant and you need to look out for the signs (pp.152–3).

Pregnancy and prenatal care

Dogs are pregnant for 63 days but be prepared for puppies to arrive a few days either side of this as the exact date depends on when fertilisation actually occurred. During this time your dog will need extra attention.

Early signs

Let your vet know early on that you have had your bitch mated; he or she will be an invaluable source of advice throughout your bitch's pregnancy. Only your vet will be able to accurately diagnose whether your bitch is pregnant during the early stages. If you can wait, you should be able to see for certain about five weeks into the pregnancy. Indicators that a dog is pregnant include a darkening and enlarging of the teats, light vaginal discharge, and abdominal swelling. If your bitch has already had previous litters, her breast development may begin only in her last week of pregnancy. If she is carrying only one or two pups, or is plump anyway, the pregnancy may be difficult to spot. Some bitches appear to "drop" overnight as they suddenly change body shape.

Other changes to look out for are nausea and increased urination. It is also very common for bitches to undergo changes in their coat, with many dogs looking particularly glossy during pregnancy. Your bitch may also display unusual behaviours, such as digging or scratching. These are

> "Only your vet will be able to accurately diagnose whether your bitch is pregnant during the early stages."

▲ **Digging behaviour**
Dogs will often show an urge to dig which may increase as they near the end of their pregnancy; this is a natural instinct.

perfectly normal as your dog is planning where she is going to have her litter and she should not be punished. Make sure she has an outlet for this urge such as newspapers indoors or a grassy area in the garden.

Care during pregnancy

It is important to take extra measures to keep your bitch parasite free to ensure that she doesn't inadvertently pass any infestations on to her puppies. Your vet will be able to advise you on the best method of treatment for pregnant bitches. There is no need to increase the amount of food your dog eats in the early stages of pregnancy. However, at around six weeks the food needs to be increased by about 10 per cent

each week. At this time your dog's exercise requirements are also likely to change. Shorter, more frequent walks that avoid very energetic activities are best. Particularly as she nears the end of her pregnancy, your dog may be reluctant to go far from home, though she will still need frequent trips outside to relieve herself.

Preparation for whelping

Long before your dog is due to have her puppies, set up a whelping area. The location of this is vital.

There should be no need to supplement your pregnant dog's food with additional vitamins as long as the food is of a high quality, but you will need to gradually increase the quantities.

It should be in the house so that your dog feels comfortable and the puppies get used to everyday household noises. However, it also needs to be out of the way in a place where few people will need to walk through once the puppies are born. It should be warm, dry, quiet, and draught free. Spend time getting your dog used to going into her whelping area, particularly if it is in an area of the house she wouldn't normally go.

The whelping box itself can be either shop bought or homemade. Speak to a reputable breeder to get tips on the best design for your dog. A breeder may also be able to loan you one of his whelping boxes, but extreme care needs to be taken to prevent cross contamination. The best whelping boxes are walled all the way around with a single gap to allow the bitch access. The gap needs to have a lip that is high enough to prevent the puppies wriggling out onto the floor but low enough to allow the bitch to step over easily, even when in the late stages of pregnancy. The base of the whelping box must be lined with newspaper, which can be easily replaced. To keep the puppies warm, use a heat source such as a heat lamp but fix it high enough to prevent the bitch from accidentally burning herself.

▼ Whelping area
Spend time making sure that your dog feels relaxed in the whelping area and get her used to you going in with her. Keep her favourite toys or blanket in the box to make it more inviting.

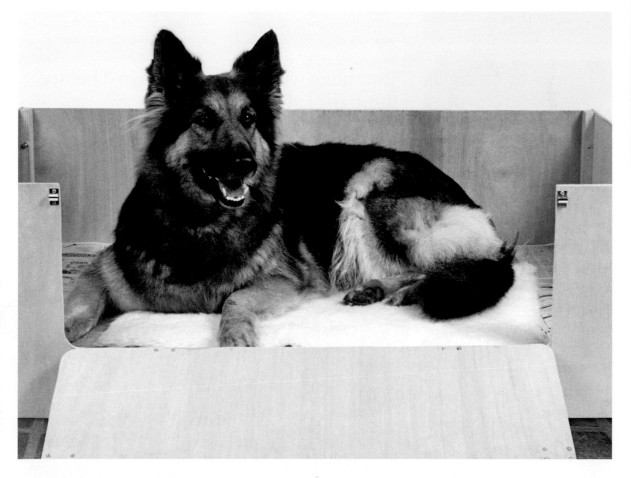

Whelping

Whelping can be a daunting prospect, however it normally occurs without any problems. The key to a smooth whelping is preparation so that you know what to expect and what to do if things start going wrong.

Whelping checklist

- A torch to keep a close eye on your bitch should she need to use the toilet.
- Clean towels.
- Spare newspapers and rubbish bags.
- Thermometer.
- Notebook and pen to monitor temperature changes.
- Disinfectant.
- Latex gloves.
- A box containing a hot-water bottle covered in a towel.
- Phone and vet's number.

Signs of whelping

As you approach your bitch's delivery date it becomes vital to keep a close eye on her. Individual bitches vary drastically in their behaviour but there are some telltale signs which you should look out for to alert you to the fact that whelping is imminent.

Approximately 24 hours before your bitch starts whelping she is likely to become restless because of the discomfort she will feel as her uterus prepares to expel the puppies. At this stage your bitch is also likely to refuse food. This is not something to worry about as she will more than make up for her lack of appetite once she has delivered all of her puppies. You may well notice your bitch begin to pant very deeply and also start to scratch and dig at the bedding of the whelping box. This behaviour originates from an instinctive desire to build a nest and should be encouraged by providing newspaper for her to rip up.

One of the most reliable indications that whelping will occur within the next 24 hours is a drop in body temperature of about 1°C (34°F). For this reason, getting your bitch used to having her temperature taken on a

▲ **Pre-labour signs**
Provide plenty of newspaper in the whelping box, which your bitch can shred leading up to the start of whelping. She may move in circles before lying down. This behaviour can continue for up to 12 hours before she gives birth.

▶ **Giving birth**
After giving birth, your bitch will strip off the membrane of the amniotic sac and sever the umbilical cord with her teeth. You should only intervene if she appears to be biting the cord too closely or pulling too vigorously.

"Your bitch will be visibly calm just before the arrival of the first puppy."

▲ Handling a newborn puppy
Take a moment to check each puppy over and rub them dry with a clean towel. Then return the pup to the mother without delay.

daily basis is good planning throughout her pregnancy. Immediately prior to whelping beginning, strings of mucus will appear from the bitch's vulva as the cervical plug that has protected the developing puppies from infection disintegrates.

The whelping process

Your bitch will be visibly calm just before the arrival of the first puppy and you should be able to see the muscles around her abdomen contract as she makes efforts to push the first puppy out. Initially you will probably only be able to see the black, fluid-filled amniotic sac, containing the puppy, appear at the vulva. Allow the bitch to stand or lie down as she prefers, but be ready to catch the puppy if it looks like it is going to drop some distance to the floor or over the side of the whelping box. If you see the puppy born with its rear end or back feet first, don't be alarmed as this is quite usual.

Normally your dog will remove the amniotic sac instinctively and begin licking the puppy to stimulate breathing. Ideally she should be left to do this herself; it is only advisable to intervene if she appears to be ignoring the puppy completely. Do not be alarmed if she starts nibbling at the puppy's stomach – she is simply severing the umbilical cord and should be allowed to do so. Once the puppy has been passed, the placenta associated with that puppy should follow. This is a good source of energy and nutrients and poses no health risks, so the bitch can eat it if she chooses. However, it is important that you count the placentas as they are passed to ensure none have been retained once whelping has finished.

The period of time to wait until the next puppy is passed can vary greatly. During that time, the puppies that have already been born should be encouraged to suckle and your bitch urged to tend to them. Take care that she does not inadvertently step on any of the puppies when giving birth to the next. If she becomes agitated, remove the puppies to a box containing a towel-covered hot-water bottle until the next puppy is born. If some time has passed, the bitch appears relaxed and she is attentive to her puppies, the whelping process is over.

Postnatal care

With the worries of the whelping process now behind you, all your focus must switch to making sure that your bitch has everything that she needs and that her puppies get the best possible start in life.

Care of the bitch

The natural maternal instincts your bitch has towards her puppies means that you will not need to do anything with the puppies initially. In fact, she will be so devoted to her puppies in the early days that you will find it difficult to persuade her to leave them even for trips to the toilet. She certainly won't need any exercise and she will only need to be taken out for short visits to relieve herself a few times a day.

Allow your bitch to do what comes naturally to her. She should periodically lick the puppies to stimulate them to pass urine and faeces, which she will consume. This process, combined with the placentas eaten during whelping, may cause your bitch to have diarrhoea, resulting in fluid loss. As a result she will require lots of water. Her food intake will also need to increase as lactation requires a huge amount of energy. It is necessary to feed about twice the number of calories she was consuming prior to whelping, and the meals need to be little and often. As she will be reluctant to leave her puppies, feeding her in the whelping box is advisable.

Care of the puppies

The puppies themselves should not be interfered with, other than to be checked over to ensure they are healthy and are putting on weight. Although born with their eyes and ears closed, puppies have a good sense of smell and will naturally navigate themselves to the teats, with gentle nudges from their mum. The bitch's first milk (called colostrum) is vital to the puppies' health and you need to be observant for any puppy that does not seem to be getting as much access to milk as the others. This means you will need to identify puppies early, either by body markings or by attaching different coloured cotton collars to each one. Take care though as puppies grow startlingly fast and will need their

▲ **Nail trimming**
Within a couple of weeks you will need to trim the puppies' nails to prevent them causing damage to their mother as they suckle.

◄ **Suckling**
The puppies get essential antibodies from their mother's first milk, which protects them against diseases. Growing pups will still need to suckle until they are about eight weeks old.

▶ **Keeping pups clean**
Licking is a hugely important activity for the health of the puppies. It cleans and stimulates the puppies and also encourages bonding between the bitch and her youngsters.

collars loosened regularly.

Be alert for any signs of a problem developing in any of the puppies, particularly in the first 36 hours after whelping. A healthy puppy is warm and dry to the touch with an elastic quality to his skin. Fading Puppy Syndrome, where puppies get progressively weaker soon after whelping, often results in the puppy dying. It may be kinder to call for your vet to humanely euthanize the pup to prevent prolonged suffering. Healthy puppies are constantly moving and twitching so if any of them are totally still or are making noise incessantly, call a vet immediately.

Tips on bottle feeding

- Only bottle feed puppies as a last resort.
- Buy a special pet feeding bottle or premature baby bottle from a pet shop or your vet.
- Stimulate the puppy to pass urine and faeces before feeding.
- Use a formula with a high protein and fat content. Ask your vet if you are not sure which brand to use.
- Sterilize all bottle-feeding equipment before each use.

Early puppy care

By the time the puppies are a few weeks old, you will constantly have them at your feet and their care becomes a full-time job. This is the most important time of the pups' lives and there is much to prepare them for.

The first few weeks

The puppies will soon begin to develop teeth, at which point their diet should be supplemented with solid food as well as plenty of chew toys to help the teething process. Introduce solid food slowly and in tiny quantities at first so that the puppies get used to digesting it. Make sure you buy specially formulated puppy food, which is high in energy with the correct balance of nutrients (p.36). Your bitch will need some time away from the puppies as her feeding responsibilities dwindle. This will also speed up the weaning process, getting the puppies used to being away from their mother. Up until now your bitch will have kept the puppies clean, so expect much more mess as you begin weaning the puppies. Use a warm damp cloth to clean their faces and fur.

Newborn development

All puppies develop very quickly in their first two months of life. No matter what their size or breed, puppies go through the same stages during their development at roughly the same time.

One week
Although born completely blind and deaf, puppies have a keen sense of smell and can easily locate their mother's teats to get food, warmth, and the comfort of snuggling up with the rest of the litter. During the first week they can't regulate their body temperature and will spend most of their time sleeping and suckling.

Two weeks
By the time a puppy is two weeks old, his eyes are starting to open but cannot focus properly. He is more active but is still unable to walk and will spend long periods sleeping.

Three weeks
By three weeks a puppy can see and hear well. He is gaining in strength rapidly and is starting to use his legs to support his body weight. He may even have started teething.

Eight weeks
Now independent of his mother's milk and with the necessary social skills for living in the company of others, an eight-week old puppy is ready to leave his mother and siblings behind and start a new life as a member of a human family group. As a responsible breeder, you need to make sure that each puppy goes to a suitable, loving home that is well prepared to take care of all his needs.

Four weeks
At this stage a puppy will start to play with his siblings, which further increases muscle strength. He will also become more vocal and growl during play. You may even hear an occasional bark.

Six weeks
Although still needing plenty of sleep, a six-week old puppy has all his milk teeth and is already eating solid food. He is keen to learn about his surroundings, which he does by exploring, sniffing, and chewing.

◄ **Socializing**
Basic training is a fun and easy way to interact with young puppies who are extremely responsive and obedient. While introducing children, ask them to sit and offer small, tasty treats to the puppy. This will help him feel comfortable and approach people confidently.

▼ **House-training**
Get puppies habituated to using newspaper for going to the toilet. Accidents will still happen but you will be making it easier for the new owners to complete the training.

Early training

As the puppies open their eyes and ears they will become more mobile and inquisitive. At this stage it is important to include them in as many family activities as possible and help them socialize with people of all ages. Most puppies will go into a home environment and therefore, during these early weeks, getting them used to the sorts of sights and noises that accompany the daily comings and goings of a household is imperative.

The vast majority of dogs that end up in rescue shelters are those that are not adequately prepared for life outside the breeder's home. A lot of emphasis is put on the role of the new puppy owner, but by the time they collect the puppy from the breeder the main opportunity for early training and socialization has already passed. Teaching a few simple rules in the breeder's home

"Spending a few minutes every day with each puppy from your litter will allow you to train and socialize them."

can make the difference between a confident and well-adjusted puppy and one that is likely to develop behavioural problems.

It is entirely possible to train puppies before they go to their new homes so that they only relieve themselves on newspaper. This makes it much easier for the new owners to complete their house-training once they get their puppy home. In addition, spending a few minutes with each puppy every day will allow you to train them to do some basic behaviours on command, such as sit and lie down.

However, the most important factor of training is to socialize all your puppies with a range of everyday

experiences such as household noises, children playing, and all-over handling and grooming. This responsibility falls to you as the breeder, as when they are only a few weeks old, puppies will happily accept new experiences with minimal reassurance.

At around 10 weeks old, puppies become significantly less inquisitive and more wary of any novel experiences. This fear is a natural protection as they stray further from the den and further into danger, but makes the job of a new puppy owner potentially difficult. If a puppy has had good early socialization with the breeder, he will emerge from this wary stage a confident youngster.

Finding new homes

Having invested so much time in the planning and rearing of your dog's puppies, you will naturally be very attached to them. Your next responsibility is to ensure that you send them to the best possible homes.

Advertising

You are likely to want to advertise your puppies for sale locally, but also contact your country's breed societies and Kennel Club to place advertisements. Advertising thoughtfully will help ensure you get the right people enquiring. For example, consider placing an advert in your veterinary surgery as opposed to the local newsagent. Likewise, avoid free ads or online websites that are likely to attract inappropriate interest. Always remember that your safety and that of your puppies is paramount so take care when inviting unknown people into your home.

Encourage prospective owners to visit often and give them as much information as possible to prepare them. You should also inform them about inherited disorders and general care and training. It is always a good idea to refer the new owners to breed societies and ask them to join so they have a good support network throughout their dog's life. Finally, make it clear that they have the option to return the puppy to you if they can no longer look after him. Your support of new owners in these first weeks can build a lasting bond that will mean you stay in contact and get frequent updates of your puppies.

Questions to ask potential owners:

- Why do you want a dog?
- Where do you live?
- Have you owned dogs before? And do you have prior experience of this breed?
- How much time can you spend at home with the dog?
- Who will care for the dog in your absence?
- Do you lead an active lifestyle?
- Do you have other pets?
- Do you have a baby, children, or elderly relatives at home?

"Your support of new owners in these first weeks can build a lasting friendship."

Assessing new owners

Spend time getting to know each puppy's future owner so that you can start preparing your puppy for the lifestyle he is going to become a part of. If your pup is going to a family with young children it is vital to get him used to them. If you do not have young children of your own, you may need to recruit those of friends or neighbours.

▶ **Meeting prospective owners**
The way potential owners interact with a puppy can tell you a lot about them. Never be afraid to refuse to sell a puppy to anyone if you don't think they will provide a suitable home.

Lasting friendship
Take extra care when introducing children and puppies. Make sure that the child understands how to interact with their new puppy correctly and train the pup to behave appropriately around children too.

Glossary

Anaesthetic
A drug used to stop a dog from feeling pain during an operation. A general anaesthetic, usually given as a gas or injection, renders a dog temporarily unconscious. A local anaesthetic numbs a small area of the body.

Antiemetic
A medicine used to stop vomiting.

Antihistamine
A medicine used to relieve the symptoms of allergy, such as itching or sneezing.

Breed
A group of dogs that share specific aspects of appearance and behaviour passed on from one generation to the next.

Corticosteroid
A drug used to relieve inflammation, joint pain, or allergic symptoms such as itching.

Crossbreed
A dog produced from parents of different breeds. Differs from a "random-breed" dog (also sometimes called a mongrel), whose parents are of no particular breed.

Double coat
A coat comprising two layers of hair: a dense, warm undercoat, and a longer, weather-resistant top coat.

ECG
Short for "electrocardiography", a diagnostic test in which an instrument is used to record the electrical activity in the heart. ECG is used to detect problems such as an abnormal heart rhythm.

Elizabethan collar
A large, cone-shaped plastic collar that is fitted around a dog's neck and head, facing forwards. It is designed to stop a dog licking or biting wounds on its body, and is used to protect an injured area or operation site.

Endoscope
A viewing instrument including a rigid or flexible tube, often with a light and a camera at the tip, which is used to look inside body passages such as the oesophagus (gullet).

Habituation
The process of getting a dog used to a stimulus (a source of stress or excitement, such as a noisy household appliance) by gradually exposing the dog to that stimulus until he no longer reacts to it.

Hand signal
A distinct gesture used to give a dog a specific command.

Hand-stripping
A grooming technique in which dead hair is pulled out of a dog's coat either by hand or with a stripping knife; used on non-moulting breeds with a wiry top coat.

Heelwork
Training your dog to walk close by your side, either on or off the lead.

House-training
Training a puppy or dog to relieve himself outdoors rather than in the home.

Hypoallergenic diet
A restricted diet used to identify and control food allergies. Some pet food manufacturers produce special hypoallergenic foods for dogs.

MRI
Short for "magnetic resonance imaging", a medical scanning technique in which magnetic fields and radio waves are used to produce an image of internal body tissues.

Muzzle
A device made of cloth, leather, or plastic, used to stop a dog biting. It fits over a dog's nose and mouth and is fastened at the back of the head.

Neutering
The removal of a dog's reproductive organs so it cannot produce puppies. In males it involves castration (removal of the testicles), and in females it involves spaying (removal of the uterus and ovaries). Non-neutered dogs and bitches are referred to as "intact".

Pedigree
For a dog of a particular breed, the pedigree is a written record of that dog's recent ancestry. A pure-bred dog is sometimes referred to as a "pedigree" dog.

Positive training
A style of training based on rewarding only desired behaviour in a dog while ignoring unwanted behaviour.

Postnatal
A term meaning "following birth": for example, postnatal care of a bitch and her puppies.

Prenatal
A term meaning "before birth": for example, prenatal care of a pregnant bitch.

Puppy teeth
A dog's "baby teeth", like the milk teeth in a human child. Puppies lose their puppy teeth at about four to six months of age, as the adult teeth come through.

Rawhide
The tough inner layer of animal hides (such as cow, buffalo, or horse hide), used to make chewy toys and treats for dogs.

Reward
A food treat or positive attention (such as vocal praise or strokes) given to a dog when he has done something correctly.

Selective breeding
Mating particular individuals of a certain breed in order to produce a desired characteristic or to eliminate undesired or unhealthy characteristics.

Slicker brush
A brush with a wide, flat head and thin metal bristles, designed to remove dead, matted hair.

Socialization
The process of teaching your puppy to get used to new people and other animals.

Topcoat
The outer layer of a double coat, consisting of long, tough, weather-resistant hairs.

Undercoat
The inner layer of a double coat, consisting of soft, warm, dense hairs.

Vaccination
Also called immunization, a procedure used to prevent a dog from catching specific bacterial or viral infections. It involves inoculation – injecting a vaccine (a substance containing weakened or dead bacteria or viruses) into a dog. The dog's immune system attacks the organisms in the vaccine, and in so doing will "learn" to attack the actual disease organisms in the future.

Voice cue
A word or sound used when training a dog to do a specific action.

Weaning
The process by which puppies graduate from drinking their mother's milk to eating solid food. It naturally happens between three and six weeks of age.

Whelping
For dogs, the term used for giving birth.